KERN COUNTY
SPORTS CHRONICLES

COLORFUL ATHLETES OF THE CENTRAL VALLEY

BRYCE MARTIN

THE
History
PRESS

Published by The History Press
Charleston, SC 29403
www.historypress.net

Copyright © 2013 by Bryce Martin
All rights reserved

First published 2013

Manufactured in the United States

ISBN 978.1.62619.144.0

Library of Congress CIP data applied for.

To Marcy

CONTENTS

FOREWORD

The tellings in this book deal with people, places and events in Kern County, California, that might well otherwise have been lost in historical perspective. Moreover, those who have earned their journalistic chops in Kern County know that it is a unique place—no glitz, no glamour, blue-collar to the core and proud of its insularity, which has bred a tacit "us against the world" mentality.

Martin has meshed sports and journalism as his life's sustenance. His stories and subjects are diverse, sprinkled with interesting information, numerous quotes and background stories that entertain and, in many cases, provide contrast to the current norm a quarter of a century later.

Martin has written his way across the county, his trail covering connections with the *Ridgecrest Daily Independent*, the *Taft Midway Driller* and the *Bakersfield Californian*. This project is one man's body of work and certainly could prove worth its time, both to old-timers who may nod their heads in remembrance and later generations curious about "ancient" history.

—Larry Press, Retired Sports Editor for the *Bakersfield Californian*

AUTHOR'S NOTE

Each chapter in this book was gleaned from articles written by the author in publications between 1975 and 1987 (see About the Author) and from other original presentations of formerly unpublished work by the author.

Part I

EASTERN KERN COUNTY

Chapter 1

Verl Lillywhite Starred for USC, 49ers

Ridgecrest, September 5, 1978

Verl Lillywhite, Burroughs High athletic director and assistant football coach, still has his bubble gum trading card from when he was fullback for the San Francisco 49ers of the old All-America Football Conference. The sketch on the back of the Philadelphia-based and now-defunct Bowman Card Co. card reads:

> *In 4th season for the 49ers. A crushing runner. Can give top-notch performance as fullback, halfback or quarterback. Equally good on offense or defense. Named on All-Pacific Coast team while at Southern California. Played for Trojans in 1946–48 Rose Bowl games. In high school, won letters in football, basketball, tennis, and track. Runs a grocery business in Los Angeles.*

Lillywhite carried the groceries for the 49ers during a pro career lasting from 1948 to 1951. He then joined the U.S. Navy during the Korean War. His mother saved his card collection. Lillywhite has another card of himself from a different series, as well as several of his teammates and opponents. The Bowman card, No. 33, is from a series of 144 different cards issued in 1951. The full-color cards sell for one dollar each today in a hobby turned gold with a current card-collecting boom showing no sign of letup.

Collectors and autograph seekers of all ages write Lillywhite for his signature on their cards. Ex-players such as Lillywhite are tracked down, and addresses are published in the many collector magazines to alert and inform hobbyists, many of whom rely on a book titled *The Sports Collector's Bible*, crammed with 450 pages of end-all hobby information.

"I had a kid from New Jersey send his two cards of me to be autographed not long ago," said Lillywhite, speaking from his athletic department office just before it was time to send his sophomores through a game-situation scrimmage. "I've showed them to the kids a few times. And now when someone asks me to see one, I kid them and say, 'Sure, but it'll cost you a dollar.'"

Lillywhite's only other card issued was part of the 1950 Bowman set.

After hanging up his cleats for the 49ers, Lillywhite took a turn in coaching football at Chino High School, where he stayed four years. While there, he had an offer from a former college and pro teammate, Don Clark, to handle USC's head coaching position. "I didn't know if that was what I wanted," recalled Lillywhite. "I liked coaching high school and wanted to stay with it. I turned down the offer, and they hired a guy from Oregon named John McKay."

Lillywhite did eventually leave high school coaching to become head coach at Chaffey Junior College for three years and later had a six-year stint at Mt. San Jacinto Junior College as assistant coach.

While in the Southland, he joined in the broadcasting booth as a fight commentator with Bill Walsh, who now does special segments for the California Angels baseball team and was considering at the time a career in sports broadcasting.

Another sideline activity served directly in bringing Lillywhite to Ridgecrest and Burroughs High.

"Me and Bruce Bernhardi, who[m] I knew when he was at Azusa, officiated basketball games together. In 1969, when Trona was in the small schools playoffs, I said to him, just kidding, 'Hey, I got to get somewhere out of the smog.' An opening actually came up, and I've been athletic director here since 1970."

Trona, twenty-five miles east, was where Bruce and his brother, Lee, attended high school. Both played college football, Lee for the Washington Huskies and Bruce for Northern Arizona University. Lee became a magazine cover subject when he married Janet Lennon, the youngest of the singing Lennon Sisters. Bruce became head football coach at Sherman E. Burroughs High in Ridgecrest in 1967.

Lillywhite has coached two sons while at BHS. Mike, now in the U.S. Marine Corps, was a slot and defensive back from the class of '74, and Jim was an all-league quarterback his senior year in '73.

In his role as sophomore-level coach for the Burros, Lillywhite said he has never tried to play up the pro-as-future angle to either his sons or others in the program. "The big thing in school is for a young man to learn things that will help him take his place in society," said Lillywhite. "If he goes on to college to play football, that's good, too. I really enjoy working with the kids. They're people fun to work with."

Lillywhite's coaching philosophy is largely styled from the only coach he ever played under as a 49er, Buck Shaw, a former Notre Dame star. Lillywhite recalls:

> *Buck never raised his voice, but he was the kind of guy you'd run through walls for. We didn't have any contact in practice after exhibition. That was Buck. Other coaches might have you hit every day. He kept us in super shape by running, and we had very few injuries on a squad of thirty-three. Buck felt you should already know the fundamentals or you wouldn't be around long. My philosophy with the sophomores is much the same. Sometimes I think the pro game gets to be too complicated. Sometimes I think they over-emphasize too many things instead of having one thoroughly know their job.*

The job for Lillywhite in the All-America Football Conference was clear enough: help his team to a title. Shaw's team did not do bad trying, twice barely losing to the Browns, 14–7 and 17–14, for a chance at the cake. And in 1951, they lost out by a half game to the Rams for the league title. The team was led by Joe "The Jet" Perry, who rushed for over one thousand yards in 1953 and 1954 and is now enshrined in pro football's Hall of Fame in Canton, Ohio.

One of pro football's first black stars, Perry was Lillywhite's roommate. "Joe was a great player," said Lillywhite. "We played against each other when he was at Compton JC and I was at Modesto JC a year before going to USC. We had a lot of great players on the 49ers. Frankie Albert was our quarterback. Norm Standlee, an All-American from Stanford, was another. Standlee had an enormous influence on my life. He was my idol when I attended Inglewood High [California], and he was a fullback at Stanford. The war took us apart, and when we were back together again, I took his offensive job away from him and he was moved to defense. That's quite a shock to put on your idol."

His first year in the pros, Lillywhite's salary was $7,500, pale alongside today's standards. "We didn't make enough money to say we were playing for money," said Lillywhite. "We played for the fun of it. Runner-up money in 1949 was $365 per man. But it was big business. Kezar Stadium had sixty

Fullback/kicker Verl Lillywhite (71) of the 49ers tackles the Cleveland Browns' Cliff Lewis after Lillywhite's quick kick in the first quarter of the All-America Football Conference championship game at Cleveland Stadium on December 11, 1949. *Author's collection.*

thousand people every game. The players just didn't know how to bargain. Joe Perry was making peanuts. I remember a college kid doing a research paper on pro football salaries. The average lineman was making $6,500, and backs were drawing $6,700, in '51."

A five-eleven, 185-pounder, Lillywhite still held rookie status when, in 1948, he helped raise his salary by performing well enough to finish second in Rookie of the Year balloting behind Y.A. Tittle, then with Baltimore and another future Hall of Famer.

Although athletes then had yet to perfect the art of selling shaving cream and other commercial products, Lillywhite picked up some side money he was not expecting. "I was asked to write about myself for an article titled 'Impressions of a Rookie.' I did, and then I forgot about it. Then, after the article hit all the wire services, I got a check in the mail for $1,500. I took it to Coach Shaw and asked him if I was supposed to give it to the team or what. He said, 'No, keep it. That's your money.'"

Lillywhite said he was able to save $25,000 from money made during his time with the 49ers, which, unfortunately, he lost later to a bad investment. He still has his bubble gum cards, though. At a dollar a peek to view, he and his wife, Geri, might have another nest egg soon enough.

Little-known fact: In college in 1946 at the University of Southern California, Lillywhite booted an eighty-three-yard punt against Notre Dame, still a record by a Fighting Irish opponent.

Afterword: Lillywhite sent Mal Florence a copy of this story. Florence, a *Los Angeles Times* newspaper sportswriter and fellow USC alum, focused on the fact that Lillywhite and Perry were the first black and white roommates in the NFL, a fact mentioned here as more of an aside. It became the theme of an article published in *Sports Illustrated* with an assist from Florence. Norm Standlee, Lillywhite's idol, whom he replaced in an offensive slot for the 49ers, had quarterbacked Notre Dame to its first undefeated season under coach Knute Rockne. Lillywhite regularly challenged foes to racquetball matches in Ridgecrest, a sport in which he was surprisingly agile and adept for someone in his fifties, perhaps due to his natural athleticism and college tennis background. He rarely lost in any of those challenges. In the pro ranks, he had one of the oddest of all nicknames: "Giant Wallet," or "Big Wallet." He received a bachelor's degree in marketing at USC, which might help explain how he acquired the nicknames. To get some perspective on Lillywhite's era, note that another card in that 1951 Bowman series was one of rookie New York Giants halfback Tom Landry. Lillywhite was one of the rushers who helped the 49ers set an NFL record in 1948 of 3,663 yards on the ground. Verl Thomas Lillywhite passed away on July 14, 2007, in Mesa, Arizona. He was eighty years old.

Chapter 2
BARS, BOXING AND BATTLING BOZO

Inyokern, June 5, 1979

At age sixty-seven, he's still trim and looks ready to go the distance—a portion of it, anyway.

During the post-Depression days in the coal and steel town of Birmingham, Alabama, Bill Pierson was a professional boxer, just in his teens but fighting the comers of his era.

The hair now is a gray blanket, but the eyes are clear with an ever-present liquid twinkle. He doesn't talk like a former pug, and his nose is not flat, his ears not a calloused blob. Still, he was a fighter.

"I wasn't that great," he says. "I didn't go very far."

Pierson is the owner of the Sierra cocktail lounge in Inyokern, his fourteenth bar—or one fewer than a fifteen-round main event. The bar count started in 1934; he owned twelve in San Diego alone.

Today, Pierson looks more like a retired tennis pro, except for the big cigar wedged in the corner of his mouth, much like the ones all boxing types chewed on in the old movies. Pierson's west bar wall is lined with old clips and pictures from the boxing game and some of newspapermen. His Second Street San Diego bar, The Press Room, was right across the street from the *Union-Tribune* office. A former copyboy for the *Birmingham News*, he has always liked newspaper people, and they figured prominently in his early ring battles. "Fights in those days were decided on by what was called 'newspaper decisions,'" says Pierson. "The South wasn't under any association rules or rankings. Three sportswriters covered the matches, and along with the referee and judges, the majority ruled."

Pierson was sixteen when he first went into the ring. Four rounds later, he stuffed $7.50 into his pocket. "My mother's insurance man was a fight promoter," he said. "I was a scrawny kid, and I was always houndin' him to get me a fight. One day, he took me up on it." That was in 1929. His overall lightweight record was 27–3–3. His biggest purse amounted to $175.00. The gloves went into storage at age nineteen when Pierson made a clean break into the U.S. Navy.

"I worked 6:00 a.m. to 2:00 p.m. at the newspaper, went to the gym, left there for another job and was up at 4:00 a.m. for road work. I hung around the Boys Club…it was something to do. Birmingham in the '20s was a terrific fight town. It was nothing to see a crowd of ten thousand."

The only world champion to come out of the Boys Club in Pierson's time was featherweight Petey Sarron (1936). The best and most exciting period performer in Birmingham—called the "Pittsburgh of the South," says Pierson—was a light heavyweight known as Battling Bozo (Curtis Hambright). In 1930, Pierson fought a Fourth of July main event in Athens, Alabama, and drove to Birmingham afterward to be in Battling Bozo's corner when the hometown boy defeated Yale Okun.

He was once in the ring with Jack Dempsey, but not to box the "Manassa Mauler." Dempsey, recently retired, had refereed a prelim bout between Pierson and Sammy Nero—"to break in his shoes," says Pierson—before refereeing the main bout.

The most exciting boxer on the scene today, Pierson says, is Indian Red Lopez. "He gets knocked on his butt, but he's right up again. But this kid Sugar Ray Leonard will make a lot of money. He's a showman. He'll probably be champion, too, because who's he got to fight?"

Bar talk over the years has aided in reviving some of Pierson's literal past. Chitchatting in one of his San Diego bars one day about an old ring foe, Johnny Romero, brought a reaction from a counter patron. Romero had been an usher in the guy's church. Forty-four years later, the two got together and rehashed a lot of old memories.

"He was clever," remembered Pierson of Romero. "He could lie across the ropes, and you couldn't hit him. He hit me the hardest I was ever hit."

Romero, he noted sadly, died penniless, a victim of the bottle. But such is not the case with Pierson, who is not selling pencils these days from a street corner. Quitting the ring prematurely may have been his best decision of all. There were some second thoughts after his four-year military tour ended. A politician named Fred Craft had Pierson set for a six-round bout when he was called for a dishwashing job. He didn't have to think twice to figure which direction would keep starvation from knocking.

When asked what is wrong with boxing—a standard question brought forth often in the last fifteen years or so—Pierson replies, "The wrong people are pulling the strings. Boxers dodge the best opponents and move with the money until they have to fight the big one. They promote up the nothing fights. What boxing needs is a czar like baseball had with Kenesaw Mountain Landis—one man to pull the strings. You box or else."

His suggestion cannot be shrugged off lightly—not from someone who battled up the ranks from a dishwasher to start his own collection of watering spas.

Pierson and his wife, Lori—who, according to Bill, could talk boxing all day and into the dark—both say they "love the Inyokern area." Lori, short for Lorelei, worked in the advertising department of the *San Diego Union-Tribune* and met her husband at his Press Room. "You meet the greatest people in cocktail lounges," Bill says.

"An interesting thing about Bill is his will," Lori says. "He showed me the will he had made out when he was married before, and his estate went to the Boys Club in Birmingham. It still does. I was impressed with his gesture."

Pierson is concerned about his future heir, though. "I don't know if the Boys Club is still there," he says. "My attorney wanted me to list the address and phone number of the place. I called the *Birmingham News* to find out, and the guy says, 'Great story. Let me get this down.' I never did find out. There are Boys Clubs all over. Surely, a town as big as Birmingham will always have one."

With guys like Bill Pierson around, they will. And some of the boys might remember him with more regard than your average, old-time lightweight.

Afterword: Pierson passed away in Sun City, California, in 1997. "I really miss him," said Lori. "He told such wonderful stories. A lot of the boxers would come in, like Ken Norton, just to listen to him. He gave Ken some tips on fights he had coming up, and Ken idolized him." Lori maintains Uncle Bill Inc., her late husband's Boys Club fund.

Chapter 3

VEON WALKING HIS WAY TO 1984 OLYMPICS

Ridgecrest, June 15, 1979

Travis Veon admits he might look a little funny to some passersby when he's out for his daily workout. There's just something about the wiggle a racewalker has that brings out the giggles and the beeping of auto horns. "It happens all the time," the sixteen-year-old says, undaunted by any of the distractions. In fact, he can see a little humor in it himself. "Little kids really do look funny when they racewalk," Veon said.

Veon, however, is a serious competitor—make no mistake about that. One of the top racewalkers in the United States, he set a national record at age eleven when he shaved fifteen seconds off the standing record of four minutes and twenty seconds in the 880-yard walk at the Pacific Association AAU Junior Olympics held in Millbrae, California, during the late summer of 1974.

At the Mt. San Antonio track on Sunday, June 17, in Walnut for the 1979 National Amateur Athletic Union (AAU) Track and Field Championships, he will be the youngest performer there vying for a place among the top three track-and-field athletes for advancement to Puerto Rico in July for the Pan-Am Games and in August for the World Cup Games. Veon will start his twenty-kilometer walk at 7:00 a.m.

In track and field since age six and a racewalker since he was ten, Veon qualified for the Pan-Am Trials at Long Beach on March 17. Ron Laird, a four-time Olympian, covered the distance in one hour and thirty-six minutes to win, and Veon was second with a personal best of one hour and thirty-nine minutes. The qualifying standard for the Pan-Am Trials is one hour and forty minutes or better, Veon said. "I went pretty hard in that one," Veon says, "but it wasn't a good time for Laird. Still, I wasn't close to him. He will be much lower than one hour and thirty-six [minutes] on Sunday."

About the race Sunday, Veon adds, "I won't be in it, really. Sure, I'd like to go as far as the Olympics someday, but that's far away. It'll be a long time before I'm an American-class walker."

He might be right about "not being in it" Sunday. The twenty-kilometer racewalk field includes Larry Walker, a five-time Olympian; Todd Scully, who was in the '76 Olympics; Neal Pike, who has a pending American record in the 20K; and Laird. The premier racewalker, though, is Raul Gonzalez, the holder of all world records with the exception of the 20K.

In preparation for junior national racewalking events, Travis Veon concentrates on his form in walking ten to fourteen miles a day on Ridgecrest roads. *Author's collection.*

"I should make my big showing in the Junior Nationals in the 10K," says Veon. "If I do okay there, I'll go on to compete in the USA-USSR track-and-field meet." The Junior Nationals will take place in Bloomington, Indiana, on July 22–24. Last year, Veon was in the meet and placed sixth.

A cross-country runner at Burroughs High and for the AAU Maturango Milers in past years, Veon says he will drop all future running events. "Racewalking and running are diametrically opposed," he says. "In this country, racewalkers still do some running, but it is going out of style. You shouldn't run at all. This was my last year in cross country."

A racewalker gets just as tired afterward as a runner, according to Veon. "You get very tired. You don't use your cardiovascular as much while walking, but you're winded at the finish. It may not be faster, but walking is more natural than running, and it feels better to walk."

Veon says it is not hard to get the technique down, although walkers are often disqualified for not having one foot on the ground at all times. He has never been disqualified, but he has had two warnings. "Both times it was in the mile walk and from the same judge," he said. "And it was illegal both times. I started off too quick and was off the ground. Veon adds, "Walkers are usually disqualified because they can't maintain. You have to relax and work at the same time. It's difficult. You can't walk when you're tired. I've got the form down, but if I tie up [muscle cramp], I have a problem. I have to cope with it. There's no way I can adjust automatically."

Veon's only coach has been his father, Roland, a track coach for Burroughs High and the Maturango Milers. His first racewalk was the result of an accidental introduction. "I was seven and in a junior meet here in Ridgecrest when we saw 'racewalk' on the program," Veon says. "We thought it meant that you would run and then walk when you got tired. After it was explained, I tried it and liked it. It was about four years later before I could find anyone to walk against again."

Now he is the only racewalker in town. Why is that so? "People say you look funny," says Veon, supplying one possibility. "They watch and think it's kind of funny, so they stay out of it. But it's getting big, especially on the East Coast. I'd say in the next three years, it will be very popular."

LIKES "TEAM CONCEPT"

July 11, 1979

At Walnut, Veon finished twentieth, clocking in at 1:42:15, backing up his "I won't be in it" claim. Still, it's not bad considering the top-rung competition he was up against. Being part of a team is something he values as much as his personal goals and achievements.

Some might want to eliminate team scoring from international and Olympic track competition, but as far as Veon and the rest of the United States Junior Track Team are concerned, having their team win a meet is a big thrill.

"That was the biggest thing I got out of being part of the United States team," Veon said, regarding the 10K walk he and team members participated in at various venues. "Everybody got at least one point as long as you finished the race. Everyone felt useful working together as a team. We really wanted to beat the Russians badly, especially since we lost at Bakersfield. We did a lot better in Boston."

The Soviet Union won the meet in Bakersfield on June 28–29. Last week, the United States came back to capture the Boston meet. The Soviet Union was led by Andrey Perlov and Vladimir Pishko.

Veon, a five-foot-seven, 130-pound high school junior, finished third in each meet and beat out teammate Tim Lewis of New York both times. Veon's time in Tulare (the walk for Bakersfield was held there) was 48:41.97. He recorded a 51:37.6 time in Boston. Lewis's Boston time was also much slower than his Tulare clocking.

"I don't know why our times were slower in Boston," Veon said. "The Russians were faster there."

Veon maintains a narrow lead over two Soviet Union competitors in Tulare, California, in a qualifier event for the upcoming AAU Junior Nationals in Bloomington, Indiana. *Author's collection.*

Veon, the youngest member of the U.S. men's squad, liked the junior national meet in Bloomington better than the Tulare and Boston meets. "They had a really nice track in Bloomington," he said. "The one in Tulare was a good one but not as good. The Boston track was only 398 yards [compared to the usual 440 yards]. I wasn't used to it."

Qualifying for the junior team was a high point, but a "flat tire" could have derailed that achievement. A lanky walker stepped on Veon's foot at Bloomington, and his shoe came off. He had to stop and put it back on and catch up with the rest of the field. "The Russians were very good," said Veon. Thanks to a high school Russian-language course, Veon acted as the speaker when it came to bartering souvenirs with the Russians.

Veon received his private pilot's license at age sixteen and pilots his father, Roland, to regular AAU meetings in Tulare. "It is a big help," said Roland. "It shortens the time I would have had to have by driving the distance." Roland, a data analyst for the Naval Weapons Center, has a math degree from Cal Poly-Pomona and coaches high school track and field.

The young Veon is attached to two primary track clubs, the Maturango Milers in Ridgecrest and the Los Angeles–based Bauchet Street Walkers. The latter is an AAU club formed by Sheriff Ed Bauldin, a friend and fellow racewalker. Bauchet Street is a high-crime district in Los Angeles frequented by real streetwalkers and is also home to a jail. Bauldin apparently has a sense of humor.

Veon had his fastest time at Bloomington, 48:20:3, losing to Lewis, who set a meet record with 48:12:2. He said his plan now is to take it easy for a while. "I generally average around ten to fourteen miles of walking a day," said Veon. "You can't keep it up all year. I'll probably start walking again seriously at the beginning of next year. I want to get ready for the next junior meet by participating in a few events early next year." He has the 1984 Olympics in Los Angeles on his mind, but for now he is content on making the junior national team. "I would like to make the junior national team for four years," said Veon. "I know it will be hard to make the Olympic team in 1980."

Afterword: Travis Veon was hit by a car while in a pedestrian crosswalk during his senior year at Burroughs High. He suffered a broken leg and never competed seriously again in racewalking. His racing counterpart, Tim Lewis, made the 1988 Olympic squad. Travis earned a degree in aerospace engineering from Cal Poly-Pomona. He and his wife, Ilka, reside in Rancho Cucamonga, California.

Chapter 4
MARK POHL: MODERN PENTATHLETE

Ridgecrest, 1978

No, Mark Pohl has never met Olympic decathlon champion Bruce Jenner. But he doesn't expect people to stop asking if he has when they find out he is a modern pentathlon athlete.

Only sixteen, Pohl was sixth best in the country in 1978 in the junior modern pentathlon events held on July 8–15 at Fort Sam Houston, Texas.

"It's called modern pentathlon because the pentathlon is a women's track event…all track," explained Pohl. "The modern pentathlon is five different sports: riding, fencing, shooting, swimming and running. Still, people get them mixed up, or they think it's the decathlon and ask if you know Bruce Jenner."

The modern pentathlon has been a part of the Olympic Games since 1912, when it was reintroduced by the founder of modern Olympics, Baron Pierre de Coubertin. It was introduced in 708 BC in the Olympics by the Spartans.

Pohl, on the Burroughs High swim and cross-country track teams, has ambitions aimed at World Team and Olympic international competition. He's already had a taste.

While in Texas this year with the National Training Squad, the Olympic Committee flew Pohl and his teammates to Colorado Springs, Colorado, for the ABC-televised Sports Festival during the latter part of July. Pohl competed against Olympic members and was shown on the *Wide World of Sports* program in the one-thousand-meter equestrian event. And as if that wasn't enough in one day, the slender horseman was rated a "perfect ride" for his debut with Olympic-caliber competitors. He even shot a game of eight ball with world-class sprinter Harvey Glance while on free time in the high country. Bruce Jenner, however, was nowhere to be seen.

Young Pohl's interest in sports goes clear back to infancy—sort of. At about eighteen months, his parents, Lloyd and Edella, took him to an orthopedist when they became concerned about the infant's lower limb development. Mark does not remember that, of course, but he does remember a later doctor telling him he would never be much good in sports, not even with a shoe correction, because he had flat feet and knock-knees.

"Mark went out to prove him wrong," said Edella, who flew to Colorado with her husband to witness her son's performance. "Mark has been training since he was six. He started out in judo and did quite well. Then, when the local judo died out, he went into other things."

"I'm still pigeon-toed though," Pohl reminded her.

The future Olympic hopeful started his real interest in the modern pentathlon when he came across a magazine article regarding swimming and running combinations. His coach, Roland Veon, felt Pohl had a good swim-run compatibility. A letter of application to the Modern Pentathlon Training Center was returned with questions toward qualification entry.

"They can't take a million people," Pohl said, "so they ask you to turn in your best times in the 300-meter or the 326-yard swim. They pick you from that information."

There is no cost for Training Squad members, except for food. Board is free, and it is a barracks-life atmosphere at the Fort Sam Houston army post, where Pohl has lived most of the past three summers.

Pohl was a novice during Clinic Championships his first year in 1976. The next year, as a junior member, he placed third in clinic trials and twelfth in nationals. His finish this year was just two points away from the next highest finisher, who, along with the rest of the top leaders, went to Jonkoping, Sweden, where competition started on August 19 for the World Modern Pentathlon Championships.

Fencing is Pohl's weakest event; he piles up most of his points in swimming and running. "I don't get much fencing practice around here, that's the reason why," he said. He practices .22-caliber pistol shooting at the local gun club. About a month before flying away to Lone Star plains, he took several riding lessons. At five feet, nine inches and weighing about 150 pounds, Pohl is about the right size for the pentathlon. After 170 pounds, he says the horse riding may present a problem.

Competing over a five-day period, pentathletes are judged on how well they ride a horse, selected by lot, over a one-thousand-meter course with a variety of jumps and obstacles. In fencing, an electric épée is used, each contestant facing another in one-touch, three-minute contests. Next comes shooting a .22-caliber pistol at a turning target. After a three-hundred-meter swim, the last event is a four-thousand-meter cross-country run.

"He puts in hours a week all year long," said Edella, looking across the Pohl living room, where her son sits on the sofa with a fencing outfit given to him by the Olympic Committee. "I hope it pays off for him. Not financially, but pride wise."

Pohl was one of only sixty U.S. athletes training for the Modern Pentathlon, and just four spots were available on the Olympic Team. A misconception about the sport is that you have to be in the army to compete in the event. It is true that prior to World War II most of the competitors were military personnel. In addition to the army post at Fort Sam Houston, the only other training facility was operated by John DuPont at his eight-hundred-acre estate in Newtown Square, Pennsylvania.

Afterword: As a senior at California State University at Long Beach, Pohl was a top épéeist. The leader in his conference, he earned All-American honors in the NCAA championships. ESPN covered the 1980 NCAA Fencing Championships, in which Pohl was one of the top twenty-four men's épée fencers in the nation. In 1983, in the twenty-one-and-under Junior World Modern Pentathlon Championship held in Coto de Caza, California, Pohl placed fifth overall, the top showing for any American. He made a serious attempt to qualify for the Olympic team when he spent the entire year of 1987 training at Fort Sam Houston. He just missed making the 1988 team. "It was my pinnacle," he says. Based now in Walnut Creek, California, Pohl is still competing. In early December 2012, he was in Milwaukee qualifying for the 2013 Senior World Championships. Pohl placed seventh in the veteran men's (age fifty to fifty-nine) épée.

Chapter 5
JAY CARTY: LAKERS GREYBEARD ROOKIE

Ridgecrest, February 9, 1979

So far, the life story of Jay Carty has been one of unexpected happenings. Take, for instance, the year 1968, when at age twenty-seven, he was the oldest rookie in the NBA. That was ten years after the Burroughs High grad was an All-CIF North-South first-team pick headed for Oregon State at Corvallis. Burroughs had nipped Bell Gardens 41–40 in the CIF championship playoffs in 1958 to cap a 21–3 season and the CIF Northern Division cage crown.

Carty, a six-foot-six, 165-pounder, was the only player in the Desert-Inyo League with the ability to dunk the basketball. He was joined on the All-CIF team by Carl Hall of Trona, a second-team selection.

What took Carty so long to break into the pro ranks? Did he hit all the camps as a walk-on year after year? Did he call all the NBA general managers around Christmastime and ask how their kids were doing? Did he die when tuning in to Chick Hearn's graphic play-by-play commentary?

Jay Carty didn't give any of it a thought.

At Corvallis, he did well enough in the Pacific-8 Conference that the old St. Louis Hawks made him a fifth-round draft choice in 1962. But Carty was concerned only with entering UCLA and working toward his doctorate. "I didn't sign with the Hawks because I didn't have my doctorate yet, and I was freshly married," recalled Carty, who harbors no regrets about that decision, even if it did mean passing up the chance to see how he would fare with such established Hawk stars as Bob Pettit and Cliff Hagan. "It didn't seem like a good thing to do to my bride, so we stayed and got an education," said Carty, now the director of the Alpine Covenant Conference Center in the mountain community of Blue

Carty shows he can rise to the occasion in a contest against Baltimore Bullets and former Duke University star Jack Marin (24). *Author's collection.*

AT ATLANTA						
LOS ANGELES (121)			**ATLANTA (111)**			
	FG	FT	Pts		FG	FT	Pts
Carty	2	4- 4	8	Beaty	14	5- 6	33
Cham'lain	2	3- 4	7	Bridges	2	10-10	14
Counts	6	4- 5	16	Caldwell	6	2- 2	14
Crawford	4	2- 4	10	Guerin	0	1- 1	1
Egan	1	1- 3	3	Hazzard	4	2- 4	10
Erickson	14	2- 3	30	Hudson	14	4- 5	32
Hawkins	5	2- 3	12	Ohl	1	1- 3	3
Hewitt	3	0- 0	6	Silas	2	0- 1	4
West	10	9-11	29				
				Totals	43	25-32	111
Totals	47	27-37	121				

Los Angeles	29	34	26	32—121
Atlanta	29	25	26	31—111

Fouled out—Erickson, Hazzard. Total fouls—Los Angeles 24, Atlanta 26. A—7,140.

Box score for Jay Carty's best outing of the season for the Los Angeles Lakers. *Author's collection.*

Jay, near Lake Arrowhead, where he resides with his wife, Mary, a Burroughs High grad, and children, John and Kim.

Carty did fulfill that early promise, although it was never his ambition to play pro basketball. The rookie greybeard, now six-foot-eight and 220 pounds, spent the entire season with the 1968–69 Los Angeles Lakers.

"I came in the back door," said Carty. "I was working out daily with the Bruins…I was playing some summer ball, doing well, and the Lakers had a bad rookie crop—there weren't very many of them. They offered me ten dollars a practice if I'd work out with their rookies. I ended up getting a contract."

Carty's "biggest" game with the Lakers was an eight-point, four-for-four-from-the-line performance against the Hawks in Atlanta.

Why would the Lakers sign an aging player, long away from the college-court whirl, for less than a pivotal role in team development? "I was cheap, and I was white," said Carty.

As for the reason he played just one NBA season, Carty offered, "I was going to get traded to Cincinnati, and by that time, I had two children. I probably could have been a ten-minute-a-game man for somebody, but you'd have to bounce around the teams a little before you found your niche. I wasn't prepared to do that with two children."

At UCLA, Carty was freshman coach Gary Cunningham's assistant and head coach John Wooden's part-time assistant. Cunningham is now, of course, the head Bruin basketball coach.

"I was there by the gym, and I just walked in," said Carty. "Having coached at Oregon State, I figured I'd be bored part of the time at UCLA if I stayed out of it. So they put me to work."

Carty worked with such freshmen as Lew Alcindor, soon to become Kareem Abdul-Jabbar, the 1969–70 NBA Rookie of the Year; Steve Patterson; and Curtis Rowe. The freshman team beat the varsity in its annual game.

"I was Alcindor's punching bag," Carty said. "Every time we did anything that was contact work, I played against him. There wasn't anybody else around that was going to give him any competition in practice. He wasn't going to get it against freshmen. At least I could work with him and tell him what he was doing right and what he was doing wrong."

And one of the things Alcindor was doing wrong—for a big man, anyway—was using a fade-away jump shot. Carty worked with him individually for a half hour before each practice. "We'd work on various things—his jumping, for one, and his sky hook," Carty recalled. "He had a fade-away jump shot when he came to UCLA. We did a lot of footwork drills and worked on hooks, moving across the center and getting rid of the fade on the jump shot so that he was jumping straight up and able to follow his shot. He was always responsive. I never asked him to do anything he couldn't do."

Still around his Lakers playing weight—or perhaps more appropriately, his Lakers sitting weight—Carty says of the team his former teammate Jerry West now coaches, "I don't keep up. No, not at all."

As for the Bruins, "I'll go down and see two [games] this year," he said.

Carty had dinner with Cunningham recently and frequently sees his former Lakers roommate, Keith Erickson, but he says he's primarily given up living in that past part of his life. He does have fond memories of his playing days, however. "Sure, it was fun," he said. "I got to travel, see the country, enjoy the guys and get paid, and it provided my wife and I a down payment on a house and some furniture. But I gave all that up. Now I run the conference center and have a speaking ministry. As a matter of fact, I'll be in Ridgecrest in March. They're opening a teen center at the fairgrounds, and I'll be one of the speakers there."

Carty gives credit to Burroughs High coach Bill Moore for his own development as a basketball player. Moore, he says, transformed him from a hesitant, slow and weak-shooting player into a versatile offensive threat. "Bill taught me lots of spin shots—four or five kinds of hooks from various positions that are known as junk shots," he said. "That's a compliment, though. There aren't very many players who know how to shoot junk. When you can't jump very well and you're not very fast, you have to learn how to get the ball up however you can. Bill taught me how to shoot off of either foot and with either hand and how to go to the basket in both directions. He taught me to be a versatile ball player."

Carty says Jerry West was the best basketball player he's ever seen. "West was the best. We had three superstars. Elgin Baylor was in his waning years, and Wilt Chamberlain couldn't do all the things West could."

Oregon State's Jay Carty wins a rebound battle against Ken Maren, six-foot-seven center for the Idaho Vandals. *Oregon State University*.

Even with three superstars on the roster, the Western Division champion Lakers could not stop the Celtics from winning the 1968–69 NBA crown. Ridgecrest's Jay Carty is seated next to Wilt Chamberlain on the bottom row, far right. *Author's collection.*

Even with three superstars, the Lakers, although they won the Western Division, couldn't stop the Boston Celtics from winning the 1968–69 championship.

Asked if Lakers coach Bill van Breda Kolff had a volatile personality, as it appeared on televised games, Carty said, "No. He was an easy guy to get along with. We didn't agree in terms of philosophy—in basketball or lifestyle—but he was a pleasant enough guy."

On the thought of Jerry West becoming a coach: "Never thought of it. It was never a consideration on my part."

On Chamberlain's alleged comeback: "I would doubt it."

Carty said he accepted Christ when he was fourteen but lived the life of a "Secret Service Christian." About eight years ago, however, he decided to show his badge and wear it wherever he went.

Afterword: Carty has written several books, including one he co-authored with legendary UCLA basketball coach John Wooden entitled *Coach Wooden's Pyramid of Success.* His fun and exciting outlook on life is in tune with someone who was born on the Fourth of July (1941). He was listed as a forward in his twenty-eight NBA games. Interesting is the fact that in the '62 draft, Carty went ahead of the seventh-round selection Gary Cunningham of UCLA. Carty's Lakers uniform number was 52. That number was passed on to Happy Hairston when Carty left. Carty first wore number 34, a number orphaned when its owner, center-forward Erwin Mueller, was traded on September 22, 1968, to the Chicago Bulls for Keith Erickson. Carty switched to number 52 when its wearer, forward Dennis Hamilton, left it behind after joining the Phoenix Suns in an expansion draft. Carty debuted with the Lakers on October 25, 1968. He and his wife, Mary, live in Santa Barbara, California.

PIPELINE TO OREGON STATE

In addition to Carty, two Bakersfield-born athletes played basketball collegiately at Oregon State and went on to have outstanding NBA careers: Freddie Boyd and Lonnie Shelton.

In football, Burroughs High's Pete Pifer was a bruising starting fullback for Oregon State for three seasons (1964–66). Pifer was awarded the Voit Memorial Trophy as the most outstanding player on the Pacific Coast in wrapping up his career for the Beavers. He was drafted by the New York Giants in 1967 in the eleventh round (#265 overall).

Carty was a car salesman at a time when his father, Jay Sr., was part owner of a Ford dealership in Ridgecrest. It was then that he got a chance to see the five-foot-nine, 210-pound Pifer in action for the Burros under Coach James Riley. Carty was impressed. Once back in Corvallis, he made it a point to seek out Beavers football coach Tommy Prothro regarding the bulky fullback with the short-shorn haircut.

Regarding Kern County and its assortment of athletes, Prothro had some familiarity. North High and Bakersfield College standout Vern Burke had recently graduated as an All-American end.

"I was back at Oregon State coaching the basketball freshmen when I asked the football staff to look into Pete at Ridgecrest," said Carty. "They did and came back saying he looked okay but was maybe a little slow and fat. I told them, 'Hey, the guy is five-foot-ten or so, but he can do a two-handed dunk standing flat-footed. He's an athlete.'" At OSU, Pifer became the first conference player to twice gain more than one thousand yards in a season.

North running back Pete Pifer (48) of Oregon State and Burroughs High in Ridgecrest breaks away for a short gain against the South in the January 6, 1967 Hula Bowl held in Honolulu. *Author's collection.*

Ralph Krafve, one of the all-time top Bakersfield high school basketball coaches, helped create a pipeline from Bakersfield to Oregon State. It started with Boyd (1969–72), Don Smith (1974–77) and then Shelton (1973–76). Smith arrived in 1973 but sat out a spell over eligibility issues. Next came six-foot-two Foothill guard James Childs, who lettered one year for the Beavers in 1978.

Boyd came in under Coach Paul Valenti (1965–70) and finished with longtime taskmaster Ralph Miller (1971–89). Boyd was a Round 1 selection (fifth overall pick) in the 1972 NBA Draft by the Philadelphia 76ers. The New York Knicks chose Shelton in 1976 in Round 2.

Smith, a six-foot-seven forward, was selected by the Portland Trail Blazers in Round 7 in 1977.

Shelton prepped at Foothill High, and both Boyd and Smith played at East Bakersfield under Krafve, himself an Oregon State graduate and the main link between Coach Miller and the Beavers and Bakersfield basketball talent.

Krafve fashioned a 262–56 overall ledger with four Central Section championships in thirteen seasons at East. He then moved on to Bakersfield

After ending his college basketball career at Oregon State, East Bakersfield High's Freddie Boyd was a Round 1 selection in the 1972 NBA draft by the Philadelphia 76ers. *Author's collection.*

College, where he won a state junior-college championship in 1978. His teams at BC totaled 117 wins in his first five years there.

Boyd was an assistant coach at OSU for a period after Jim Anderson took over for Miller in 1990.

In addition to Shelton and Boyd, four other former NBA players—Robert Swift, J.R. Henderson, Winston Crite and Chris Childs, younger brother of James—were born in Bakersfield, but none took the Oregon State University route. Swift did not attend college.

While Krafve posted an enviable slate, Joe Dominguez, a native of Grants, New Mexico, holds the Kern County record for the most high school basketball victories as a coach, 377. He was 20–7 in one year at Burroughs High in Ridgecrest and then compiled a 357–153 record in twenty seasons as head coach at East High School. His final team went 29–4 and won the CIF Division II title in 1993–94.

Foothill High and Oregon State basketball standout Lonnie Shelton was an NBA draft choice by the New York Knicks in 1976. *Author's collection.*

Afterword: Shelton and Boyd joined forces with Buzz Caffee, Foothill high basketball coach, in a business venture in 1980. The trio opened The Second Sole at Ming Plaza in Bakersfield, a store specializing in resoling tennis shoes.

Chapter 6
A SHORT, RECORD-SETTING NFL CAREER

Ridgecrest, 1987

At six-foot-two and 190 pounds, Mike Waters was a fluid and speedy runner with a classic, knees-high running style for the Burroughs High Burros. He was very good on the gridiron, good enough for the New York Jets to choose him in the ninth round of the 1985 NFL Draft. The Jets released him without making the squad. Showing good hands and blocking ability in camp with a new club, Waters made an extraordinary rise from free agent to starter after signing with the Philadelphia Eagles.

Waters, the son of Robert Waters, an employee in the U.S. Naval Weapons Center's Public Works Department, played well in preseason games with the Eagles. Against the San Diego Chargers, he caught his second touchdown pass of the exhibition season and carried the ball three times from the fullback slot during August 1986.

In lining up as a starter in the season opener against the Washington Redskins, Waters followed Jay Carty as the second Burroughs High grad to participate at a major professional sport level.

Robert Michael Waters, born on March 15, 1962, in San Diego, graduated from Burroughs High in 1980 when John Higdon was head football coach. After an All-Golden League senior season at Burroughs, Waters joined the Bakersfield College Renegades football team under Coach Gerry Collins. It was a storied program Waters was entering. The Renegades were national champions in 1953, 1959 and 1976. After earning all-league recognition as a running back at BC, Waters headed to San Diego State. As a senior, Waters was the leading rusher on a 4–7–1 Aztecs team that featured quarterback

Todd Santos and receivers Webster Slaughter and Vince Warren. Waters's total of 704 rushing yards was fourth best in the Western Athletic Conference.

With the Eagles, the usually quiet redhead inexplicably ruffled some feathers with comments made before a big rivalry contest involving the Eagles and Chicago Bears.

After a tough 13–10 overtime loss to the Bears, Eagles coach Buddy Ryan was his usual feisty, outspoken self. That was expected from Ryan, but rookie Waters did not fare as well in imitating the actions of his boss in the days leading up to the contest.

Ryan announced after the game that Michael Haddix would be the starting fullback the following Sunday against Denver. Waters, the fullback who had called the Bears "pansies" and "babies" the week before the matchup, was benched after three plays in Sunday's game and demoted. "He wasn't doing the job," the coach said. "Haddix probably saved his life."

The rookie fullback started against the Bears, but Ryan pulled him after the first series, and he never returned. Meanwhile, Haddix had one of his best games as a pro, running for thirty-four yards on nine carries and catching four passes for twenty-seven more.

When asked by the press why he had removed Waters so early, Ryan snapped: "Because he wasn't doing the job. He wasn't blocking who he was supposed to, so you don't fool around with people. You get them out of there. If you're gonna talk, you better be ready to back it up. I don't mind a guy talking, but if you do, perform."

In ridiculing some of the Bears, Waters's displeasure was seemingly in how he perceived the way some of them made physical gestures to draw personal attention after plays did not go their way. A recent string of fumbles on his part and missed blocking assignments added to the rookie's woes. Placed on waivers by the Eagles, Waters managed to eventually extend his NFL career by latching on with the New Orleans Saints.

In 1987, with the Saints under Coach Jim Mora, Waters set a team record with an eighty-two-yard touchdown reception on a toss from quarterback John Fourcade against the Rams. The touchdown broke the previous Saints record of eighty yards set by quarterback Bill Kilmer to Dan Abramowicz in 1967. At the time, Waters and Fourcade were strikebreakers during a time when regular NFL players held a work stoppage. Some sportswriters said that the accomplishments of the ragtag assortment of "scabs" should be noted with "scarlet asterisks."

The NFL players' strike lasted most of the season. A crowd of 29,745 fans went to the Superdome on October 4, 1987, to watch the replacement teams play. The record-setting pass from Fourcade to Waters aided in the Saints defeating the Rams 37–10.

When the regular NFL players settled their grievances with the owners, they returned to action, and replacement fill-ins such as Waters were sent packing.

Afterword: Waters's receiving record stood until 1998, when then-Saints quarterback Kerry Collins connected with Andre Hastings for an eighty-nine-yard touchdown grab against the Cowboys. In Waters's disrespectful remarks concerning the Bears, he singled out middle linebacker Mike Singletary. Years later, Singletary teamed with a writer for his biography, *One-on-One*, issued in 2005. The co-writer? Jay Carty.

Chapter 7

CHICAGO HOOPSTERS SETTLE INTO DESERT LIFE

Ridgecrest, January 26, 1979

They left the town Billy Sunday could not shut down for one that shuts down on its own at sundown.

It is a long way removed from The Loop, Lincoln Park Zoo, the Palmer House, Lake Shore Drive and State Street (that great street), to name a few points of interest, so surely Ridgecrest must have something of its own to hold the interest of Steve Parham, Louis Reymond and Mitch "Moose" Miller.

For starters, there is basketball—something the three transplanted Chicagoans knew a thing or two about before arriving. Parham, Reymond and Miller have helped make Cerro Coso College a state cage power. Together, they average about fifty points a game for the Coyotes.

And what about California? Just the name bursts a flow of dreamy possibilities—especially to ghetto-raised Parham and Miller. California is the pie in the sky.

Some others have given the area a bum's rush and taken the next charter home after Coach John Boragno has shown them the town. Of course, Stillwater has probably experienced some of the same. The question asked most often is not why they came but why they stayed.

"I can only tell them that we live in a small community. There's no large black area, and we have a small college," said Boragno.

Parham and Reymond remember well the drive up from Los Angeles International Airport.

"I wasn't quite sure where I was," recalls Parham. "We stopped at a Denny's somewhere. Then I see this sign that says 'Death Valley,' and that just blew me out."

It probably did not help Parham's anxiety when Boragno told the two they were still an hour away—and still headed toward Death Valley. "Paul Newman and Robert Redford couldn't have done it better," said Parham, referencing the two actors who played con men in the movie *The Sting*.

"I was asleep in the back seat," remembers Reymond. "It seemed like every time we stopped, I woke up and someone would say, 'Two more hours.'" Reymond recalls his area of Chicago as "smooth, middle class and two steps from Lake Michigan. I miss the sights and a couple friends. But out here there's a lot of California and a lot of places I haven't seen. I get accustomed wherever I go."

Miller attended Martin Luther King High School and competed against Parham and Reymond, who were at Wendell Phillips High School. Miller was on the varsity team his junior and senior years. King was 11–1 in the Central Division and narrowly missed winning the title his senior year. But he says that Phillips has the kingpin reputation. "Our record is pretty much the dominant one in the Chicago area," Parham agreed. "I'm trying to be modest. When Lou was a sophomore, we finished 31–1 and were state champions. Larry Williams, now at Louisville, was on that '76 team. My junior year we finished 27–4 and lost in the semifinals. I was a backup center to Robert Byrd, who's playing for Marquette now. Playing behind Byrd really helped me. My senior year we were 30–0."

Phillips has also graduated some fine football players, most recently Greg Pruitt, and going way back, Buddy Young.

Reymond, a co-captain with Byrd his junior year, says, "Back in those days, Phillips was like UCLA in the city. You could expect the gym to be jam-packed."

"My brother Rodney is a six-foot-five pure shooter at Phillips right now," said Parham. "He's a senior wearing my old number."

One thing about Ridgecrest is that it's a safer place to live than where Parham resided in Chi Town. "It's a little bit badder than what Bad Bad Leroy Brown says," Parham said, referring to the old Jim Croce song. "He wouldn't go around Thirty-ninth and King Drive."

"It's not as bad anymore," Miller cuts in.

"Where do you live, Moose?" Parham asks, as if saying, "Speak for yourself."

Miller said he lived in the neighborhood of Forty-second and College, ten blocks from King Drive. Miller now lives in Ridgecrest with John Hall, a Coyotes teammate from New York, at the Shangri-La trailer court. Parham says he is a nomad of the desert—"Steve of Indian Wells Valley."

"I'd like to settle down here after my playing days are over," says Miller.

"Uh-oh, it's time to go," says Parham.

REYMOND EARNS STATE FIRST-TEAM HONOR

April 5, 1979

Reymond became the first Coyotes athlete to garner first-team all-state recognition, a pinnacle his coach felt he should have reached the prior season. In considering his future options, Reymond has included Cal State Bakersfield as a potential next stopping-off point.

For Reymond, recently named to the all-state Division II first team by a vote of coaches in the California Community Basketball Association, it is time to do some serious looking around.

The six-foot-one offensive leader, who was the top scorer among state first-team picks with a 23.1 points-per-game average, was in a similar situation just two years ago (1977) after being named all-city and all-state as a high school senior in Chicago.

And he does not regret the decision that led him to Ridgecrest. He was the top scorer in the Desert Athletic Conference two years running and received a co–Player of the Year award this season in the DAC. In addition to his high scoring, Reymond averaged nearly eight assists per game.

He was married in February to a Ridgecrest girl, adding some weight to his next college choice.

"I've really been impressed with the people in this town," Reymond said. "There are no hostilities, and everyone treats everyone the same. I'd like to get my mother, Mandy, to come and live out here. And when I'm about fifty," he smiled, "I'd like to come back and make it my home again."

The list of four-year colleges Reymond is considering is long and includes Wyoming, Iowa, Louisiana State, San Diego State, Fresno State and Cal State Bakersfield, to name a few. He has already slated the Cal State Bakersfield campus for a visit.

"I love Cerro Coso—the fans and the whole community, especially the Fire Mountain Foundation. They gave us so much support. They did a lot for us. And Coach Boragno…he's been my best friend. I know I'll never forget him."

Cal State Bakersfield head basketball coach Pat Wennihan would like nothing better than to see Reymond in a Roadrunner uniform next season. "All the coaches I've talked to have spoken very highly of him," said Wennihan.

The Roadrunners graduated one guard, and the other starter, Manuel Calvin, a member of Bakersfield College's state championship team two years ago, is going back to BC—to play football this time around.

"We do need a guard," Wennihan said. "We were hurt last year because our guards couldn't score. I hope this is what Lou is looking for. We'll go great guns to get him."

At Cal State Bakersfield, Reymond would be getting a full scholarship and a schedule that includes a Midwest whirl against Big Eight schools Nebraska, Kansas and Kansas State. The Roadrunners are a member of the California Collegiate Athletic Association (CCAA).

There is also the potential for a good-paying summer job in the rich oil and agricultural area of Bakersfield that cannot be overlooked. "It's pretty hard to beat ten-dollar-an-hour jobs," said Wennihan, quoting the average pay scale for oilfield work.

Reymond's Coyote and high school teammate Parham might be leaning toward a rival CCAA team, Cal Poly San Luis Obispo. Mustang coach Ernie Wheeler has put the word out that he is looking for a big man (who isn't?), and the six-foot-seven Parham is planning on giving the attractive San Joaquin Valley campus a look-see. Parham was the second leading rebounder in the state this year.

Another from the DAC making the all-state team is Kevin Gaskins of Victor Valley, who shared the league's top player award with Reymond. Gaskins was an all-state honorable mention.

Afterword: Both Parham and Reymond opted to extend their college basketball careers at high-scoring Loyola of Chicago. In the 1980–81 season, the Ramblers finished 13–15. It was tough going for the former Coyotes. Reymond came off the bench to provide a spark at times. Parham was declared academically ineligible in mid-January '81. The senior forward was a starter averaging 7.3 points and 5.5 rebounds per contest. Reymond, too, was found ineligible in the second semester. A teammate, prolific rebounder Wayne Sappleton, went on to play for the New Jersey Nets of the NBA. In 1985, Coach Boragno was named the new basketball coach at Western New Mexico, leaving behind his assistant position at Cal State Bakersfield. The Fire Mountain Foundation was established in 1977 by Cerro Coso as a nonprofit corporation related to scholarships, landscaping and outreach programs. *Cerro* is Spanish for "fire," and *Coso* is Paiute Indian for "mountain." Cerro Coso is one of three colleges in the Kern Community College District.

Chapter 8

SUPER BOWL LINEMAN HUNTS ELUSIVE CHUKAR

Inyokern, January 30, 1979

While playing college football for the USC Trojans and even long before that, Gerry "Moon" Mullins took trips to the Clodt farm in Inyokern, situated in eastern Kern County. He loved the area and especially loved chukar hunting. Hunting native chukar, an upland game bird, is demanding and challenging. A shotgunner needs to be in good shape physically to cover the rugged terrain. Being a great shot is equally important when the covey is flushed and the speedy, strong-flying partridge take flight.

Mullins, just days away from celebrating yet another Super Bowl win, had hoped to stay out of the Pittsburgh snow awhile and take in some local hunting. He has done that, but being a member of the Super Bowl XIII champion Pittsburgh Steelers also has its postgame rewards: Uniroyal has beckoned him to return to the Steel City and do some tire commercials.

"I'm hoping that when I get back to Pittsburgh, I can get the whole ball of wax," said Mullins, helping dress out the day's chukar kill at his uncle Richard Clodt's trap club in Inyokern. "That's the nice thing about winning the Super Bowl—things keep popping up."

It is an open and lucrative market for Steelers players in their home city. Almost without exception, Steelers pitch a variety of wares as often as quarterback Terry Bradshaw tosses to Lynn Swann. Mullins has lately endorsed products for Samsonite luggage, Puma shoes and A&P Auto Parts.

A six-foot-three, 245-pound veteran of eight years and now with three Super Bowl wins, including Bowls IX and X with the Steelers, Mullins is no Indian Wells Valley outsider. "I like it here; it's a change of pace," said

GERRY
MULLINS

GUARD
STEELERS

Gerry "Moon" Mullins was a key player in the Pittsburgh Steelers' four Super Bowl wins. During off-seasons, he regularly visits a family hunting site in the desert community of Inyokern in eastern Kern County. *Author's collection.*

Mullins, twenty-nine. "I've been coming up here for the past twenty-five years. Every time I come out here, it seems like there's lots of new production going on. I can remember when there was hardly anything."

Mullins, who starts at right guard on the offensive line, has another uncle, Ronnie Clodt, and an aunt, Marion Hunsaker, both longtime Inyokern residents he visits while on hunting trips in the area. He's single and lives with his parents in Pittsburgh, who also own a home in Anaheim, California. He likes the Inyokern area so well that he is the owner of forty nearly barren acres north of the trap club. "I don't know what I'm going to do with it yet," he said. "Last year, I spent the off-season in Pittsburgh playing on the Steelers basketball team. I was hoping to take a rest out here this year, go home and play a little basketball and check out a job with a coal company. I've got a lot of opportunities to think over. I guess I'll go back and stick it out in the snow." Next year, he will be aiming for even bigger game when his contract is due to expire. "I'm going to start now on negotiating for next year," said Mullins.

His Super Bowl XIII ring has not arrived yet, but Mullins does not mind waiting for the diamond-studded memento said to be worth in the neighborhood of $3,000. Some easy money that came with winning the 1976 Super Bowl, however, will elude him this time around. After winning Super Bowl X, he was chosen as a member of the Steelers Super Team for ABC's Superstars competition. Each member picked up $14,000 for competing. "I was sort of hoping I'd get a shot again, but they took one offensive lineman,

Mike Webster, who deserved it," said Mullins of the All-Pro offensive center. "He's younger, and I've already been. I believe in sharing the wealth."

Mullins said the 35–31 victory over the Dallas Cowboys should silence Bradshaw critics who try to make the quarterback out to be a tobacco-chewin', country music singin' (which he's guilty of on both counts) country bumpkin—which he is not.

"He's sharp," said Mullins. "Being a quarterback who calls his own plays is going to present certain problems anyway. He's had a bad rap from the press, and I think part of it was because he had such a big build-up coming out of college. He's the kind of guy who doesn't speak out for himself. But he's won the Super Bowl three times. That's more than anyone else."

The Steelers have never lost the big one.

To those Cowboy diehards who insist that Pittsburgh did not win the game but that Dallas blew it, Mullins, eyes glinting in the sun under a Pittsburgh auto dealer baseball cap, said, "We won the game, and that's all that's important. It'll be a controversial subject for a while, and then all the talk will go out the window."

After building a 35–17 lead with just six minutes and forty-eight seconds left in the contest at Miami, Dallas erupted for two touchdowns in the last three minutes. Earlier, Cowboy tight end Jackie Smith dropped a touchdown pass in the end zone that would have tied the game at 21.

The biggest controversy, though, was the interference call on Dallas cornerback Benny Barnes on a pass from Bradshaw to Swann. Three plays later, Franco Harris ran twenty-two yards for a touchdown, adding to Pittsburgh's 21–17 lead and opening up the game.

And if people want to talk "ifs," Mullins has a response: "Bradshaw should have been blown dead on the play when [Tom] Henderson [Cowboys linebacker] took the ball out of his hands. He was stopped before Henderson stripped him."

On that play, Dallas's Mike Hegman scooped up the ball and ran thirty-seven yards for a touchdown, making the score 21–17 in favor of Pittsburgh in the second quarter.

Mullins, who calls Southern California his true home, cast all post-mortem speculation aside Sunday when he hosted a barbecue at his parents' home in Anaheim for his Steelers teammates in Los Angeles for Monday's Pro Bowl. They included Joe Greene, Harris, Webster and Jack Ham.

Greene, a left tackle on Pittsburgh's famed "Steel Curtain" defense, paid an offhand compliment to Mullins after Super Bowl XIII when he said, "Who stood out were Bradshaw, John Stallworth, Swann and the offensive line."

Mullins came to Pittsburgh in 1971 as a fourth-round draft pick out of USC. Measuring about six-foot-three in height, his playing weight dips at times to as low as 225 pounds. He is considered undersized even at his regular playing weight of 245 pounds. Mullins has said his size is not a factor because the team emphasizes trapping and pulling, whereby speed is more important than size. A right guard most of his pro career, he also fills in at tackle and even tight end in short-yardage situations.

A little-known fact is that Mullins was Terry Bradshaw's road manager for about six weeks in the 1970s when Bradshaw gave it a go as a country music singer.

Afterword: Mullins retired in 1979 after Super Bowl XIV, his fourth, and made Pittsburgh his residence of choice. Today, the Indian Wells Valley Skeet Club, located off Clodt Road in Inyokern, is still a great place for those who relish the sport of wild chukar hunting in a rugged environment. Mullins is president of Industrial Metals and Minerals in Bridgeville, Pennsylvania. His father, Stanley, passed away in 2009. His mother, Betty, lives in Inyokern while also maintaining a home in Anaheim.

Chapter 9
NHRA RACEMASTER KEEPS CARS ROLLING

Ridgecrest, August 13, 1979

Dick Mahan's battle with the "Big C" may be over. The well-known National Hot Rod Association racemaster at least has his voice back. And what good is a racemaster without a voice?

"I'm winning," says Mahan, forty-eight. "The doctor is still getting in some practice, but nothing has shown in the last three checkups. I'm not through yet."

Mahan did lose his voice at the Winter Nationals in Pomona last year, which was cause for only minor concern at first. "I lost my voice and thought I had a virus," he said. "I did, but a further check revealed I also had cancer of the gall bladder."

An operation three months ago has apparently cleared up his problems. Now it's back to what he has been doing since the late 1950s. "A racemaster's job," he explains, "is to make sure cars are in their given place at a given time. In case of an accident or other delay, I try to make up the down time—which is usually impossible. I try to make it up to where it's no more than thirty-five minutes off."

Mahan also makes a visual check of cars and drivers for last-minute details that could be forgotten, such as a driver not fastening his seat belt or a fuel leak on the line.

"The main thing is fair play—making sure both cars start together," said Mahan.

Mahan is not sure how many miles he covers in races around the country, but his itinerary should offer a good clue. Last year, he visited (in order)

Pomona, California; Bakersfield, California; Gainesville, Florida; Baton Rouge, Louisiana; Indianapolis, Indiana; Seattle, Washington; and Ontario, California. All of his racemaster duties are with the NHRA, except for the Bakersfield March Meet, which is sponsored by Famoso Raceway.

How much does he get paid for his duties? "That's not in the program," he says. "But if it was for money, none of us in the background would be at the races."

Mahan is one of several persons in the Ridgecrest area who work on the sidelines in NHRA races held all over the United States.

The big race coming up is the U.S. Nationals, scheduled August 29– September 3 at the Indianapolis Raceway Park and Speedway. "There are a dozen nationals, but this is the big one," says Mahan, a China Lake employee when not working the car tracks. "There have been as many as 1,700 cars in this one. This year is the twenty-fifth anniversary of the U.S. Nationals."

Mahan's last duties were for the February Gator Nationals at Gainesville. He says that the satisfaction he gets from his chores is not easy to explain. "If you're not into racing…not really involved, it's hard to tell someone what you get out of it," he says. "I guess you could call it an ego thing. When drivers tell me they feel more comfortable when I arrive, it's quite a good feeling."

SHADOW OF DEATH HUNG OVER U.S. NATIONALS

September 5, 1979

"The death-marred U.S. Nationals."

Unfortunately, that may be how history remembers the twenty-fifth anniversary of the top National Hot Rod Association event of the year, but there is another side to the story, says racemaster Mahan.

"It was probably the best drag race ever held anywhere," Mahan says. "It was a well-run and well-organized event. Eliminate the heat and 100 percent humidity and, of course, the deaths, and it was an easy race to work. It flowed very easy, and we worked so well together."

Three people died and twelve more were hospitalized from crashes, overindulgence, heat prostration and assorted happenings at Indianapolis Raceway Park from Wednesday to Monday in the largest drag race held in the world. The deaths were the first at the U.S. Nationals since 1969.

"It's tragic that we killed two people and another died from the heat," Mahan says. "It's cold, maybe, but it's part of the business. We don't maim, claim and hurt people that often. I'd be a nervous wreck every time someone was hurt if I dwelled on it. We ran 1,035 cars down the track Thursday alone. That's a lot of mileage for just a few incidents. No one was killed in the last ten years. How many people get beat up in football in just one year?"

Most of the mishaps occurred in the pit area and not on the track, Mahan points out. However, two of the deaths did take place on the track. Thursday night, a girl in the pit region, with the racecar Tinker Toy, suffered a heat stroke and later expired from a cerebral hemorrhage. "She was the second from the pit to go to the hospital that night," said Mahan. "It was very hot, and a doctor told us later that the same thing could have happened to any of us."

A cameraman was hit with flying shrapnel from a crashed car driven by Frank Rupert on Saturday and was killed. It was later deduced that the danger area from the shrapnel was within three square feet. Rupert sustained two broken legs.

The other death was brought on when a motorcyclist went into a high-speed wobble at 180 miles per hour after crossing the finish line, staying up only after careening and sliding along a guard rail. When the cyclist hit the end of a turnout, he ran square into a corner.

"The bikers are neat guys," said Mahan. "They're new to our sport. Everyone was wondering how they would react, but they went on like professionals after the accident. That showed us a lot."

Mahan was one of four racemasters at Indy. He had a partner on the east side of the track where Modified, Top Fuel, Pro Comp, Comp, Pro Bike and Top Fuel Bike classes filtered onto the track.

"Indy is not shaped the same as any other track," he said. "The different classes come out from the sides and funnel in. It's impossible for one racemaster or one team to take all of it in."

One of the flukiest tragedies at Indy could almost be called a comic relief when compared to some of the worse happenings. It was supplied by a man who, sitting in the top row of the grandstand, tilted over backward from watching the Golden Knights, a parachute exhibition team, and plummeted to the ground. But that's not all; on his way down, he contacted a power line with one arm and with his free hand shocked a person in the grandstand. "He survived, and the person who had been jolted came out of it okay," said Mahan. "We had a charged grandstand for a while. No one wanted to leave it, and no one wanted to get near it."

For some, the drags were just an excuse for one long party on makeshift campgrounds bordering the track. "The 'animals' lived on the west side of the track," said Mahan. "People driving by were greeted with signs like 'Show us your ass for a beer.' It's okay, but it's a 100 percent party for them. They're at every race. Helicopters and regular police patrols kept an eye on them."

The veteran racemaster was joined by fellow Ridgecrestian Chuck Cutler in his first trip to the U.S. Nationals. Cutler helped in the staging lanes. Roberta Leighton, another from the area and a longtime NHRA worker, lent a hand in pit control.

Kelly Brown of Calabasas won the Top Fuel title Monday. Canadian Gordie Bonin earned the Funny Car victory, and Bob Glidden, from Whiteland, Indiana, glided to victory in Pro Stock.

"BIG DADDY" KEEPS ON DRIVING THE WINNERS

September 26, 1979

Don Garlits, the winningest Top Fuel driver in drag-racing history, earned his twentieth career victory in his very first trip to the Fallnationals held at Seattle last weekend.

Garlits won over runner-up Kelly Brown, whose rear end and clutch assembly exploded in what racemaster Mahan called "the biggest explosion I've ever seen in a dragster."

Brown's exploding car fired parts into the crowd and brought superficial scalp wounds to a couple of spectators.

With the win, Garlits ruined the thirty-seven-year-old Brown's bid of bettering the record of four wins in a season. Both Brown and Garlits have won four times in one season; no one has won five in Top Fuel.

Mahan said the weather "was beautiful" in Seattle, no doubt contributing to a three-day attendance of twenty-seven thousand.

A native of Seffner, Florida, Garlits, forty-seven, is known far and wide as "Big Daddy," a nickname given to him by Bernie Partridge, NHRA announcer, while on duty at the 1962 U.S. Nationals. Partridge helped form the Dust Devils Auto Club in Ridgecrest in 1951. The club held regular drag and other events at the Inyokern Airport. In fact, the first-ever NHRA divisional event was held at the Inyokern strip in 1960.

Don "Big Daddy" Garlits was given his nickname by Ridgecrest's Bernie Partridge. Some memorable asphalt drama has made him a familiar figure to Kern County drag-racing enthusiasts. *Author's collection.*

Garlits is remembered just as strongly in Bakersfield for the drama he added in a 1977 showdown.

Known reverently as the "March Meet," each year, drivers come from all over the world to participate in the Bakersfield Fuel and Gas Championships. The March 4, 1977 event pitted a rival matchup with the king of drag racing himself, "Big Daddy" Don Garlits, and two-time Bakersfield winner James Warren and his Bakersfield-sponsored "Rain for Rent" dragster. Each time Warren had won, Garlits had been chosen as the favorite going in. Garlits, in a self-imposed idle streak, decided to give the field and Warren in particular another go. The duel between Warren and Garlits built momentum early on and continued through days of qualifying right up to when the foes wheeled to the starting line. Less than six seconds after the Christmas tree light flickered green, parachutes puffed out in the distance, and Warren had defeated Garlits for the third time in a row, by less than two-tenths of a second, climaxing one of the most anticipated drag races in March Meet history.

Afterword: Problems arose in 2005 when the Federal Aviation Administration handed down a new set of mandates that their airports could no longer be used for non-aviation activity, including drag racing. The airport management and board of directors were said to be sick with the thought of having to tell the Dust Devils that their long-standing relationship would have to come to an end. But with its hands tied, the Inyokern Dragstrip, a California drag-racing staple, was no more. The Dust Devils totally disbanded a few years later, marking a sad end to an important segment of drag-racing history. Mahan was mentioned in a *Car Life* magazine article from January 1969 titled "How the Pros Compete with Javelins, AMXs." The piece's author, Allen Girdler, said Mahan's AMC Javelin was "a consistent class winner in rallies and slaloms." Three photos of the car in slalom action accompanied the article. Mahan's Javelin was supplied by Charlon & Simolon, the AMC dealer in Ridgecrest, and his tires came from A&L Tire Co. Mahan's Javelin competed in stock at drags. He was the sports director at KRCK radio 1360 in Ridgecrest, the "Tri-county Station."

Chapter 10

BUDWEISER ROCKET: BREAKING THE SPEED OF SOUND ON LAND

China Lake, August 24, 1979

For Ray Van Aken, an aeronautical engineer at the China Lake Naval Weapons Center and veteran rocket expert of twenty-eight years, the idea of working on a vehicle project designed to break the sound barrier might seem a little old hat. After all, the sound barrier was first surpassed by Chuck Yeager, who flew the Bell XS-1 at 670 miles an hour at an altitude of forty-two thousand feet on October 14, 1947, at Edwards Air Force Base in eastern Kern County.

This time around, however, Van Aken's expertise has been called upon to aid in propelling a bright red needle with three wheels, called the Budweiser Rocket, to surpass the speed of sound on land.

"The purpose of the car is to set a land speed record and to break the speed of sound on land, which has never been done before," said Van Aken, fifty-one.

Also involved with the project locally is Gene Breitenstein, a retired navy computer specialist now with Datatec Inc. Breitenstein uses the Wang computer for performance calculations.

Van Aken is lending his knowledge in such areas as aerodynamic suspension, site selection, performance calibrations, design and environmental impact studies. He is responsible for the long and slender design of the forty-eight-thousand-horsepower land rocket's v-bottom, strut fairings, vertical stabilizers and side canards, which have never before been tried on a car of this nature.

"Bill Fredrick, the designer and brainchild of this test, sought me out," explained Van Aken. "I told him some things he'd have to be

Pardon my dust. A bright red needle with three wheels and a tall vertical fin at the rear, the Budweiser Rocket packs a forty-eight-thousand-horsepower hybrid power plant to push it to supersonic speeds. *Photograph courtesy Jane Van Aken.*

careful about, which led to more and more questions. It's been a very challenging project."

Stan Barrett, thirty-six, a Hollywood stuntman who lives in Bishop, will guide the rocket-powered car at Upper Alkali Lake near Alturas, a fourteen-mile-long dry lake bed never before used in a land-speed record attempt, some day in September at a projected top speed of 740 to 750 miles per hour.

Gary Gabelich set the land-speed record of 631.367 miles per hour in the Blue Flame rocket car in 1970, but Van Aken says the actual land-speed record is a little over 622 miles per hour, based on the average of the Blue Flame's two best runs. The Blue Flame's record is considered a record for a car, which Van Aken disclaims as a dubious choice of words:

> There was some chicanery with the Blue Flame, in my opinion. To be considered a car, you need to have four wheels. Two wheels were added to the front, at the nose of the Blue Flame, more as a device than a necessary function to give it four wheels. We're more honest. We won't set a land-speed record in a car, and we're not going to try and convince anyone it is a car. It doesn't even have four wheels. Fredrick said he didn't care if the

56

Bishop, California resident and stuntman Stan Barrett sits in the cockpit of the Budweiser Rocket at Edwards Air Force Base on Monday, December 17, 1979, following his preliminary speed run of 739 miles per hour. *Author's collection.*

Budweiser Rocket sets the record for cars. When it comes to breaking the speed of sound on the ground in a manned vehicle, it doesn't matter if it is with a tricycle. If you've done it, you've done it.

The International Hot Rod Association will be the sanctioning body, according to aerodynamicist Van Aken.

"We want to go supersonic, which, of course, has never been done before," continued Van Aken. "That would be about 750 miles per hour, with the

Designer Bill Fredrick, driver Stan Barrett and owner Hal Needham make preparations to assault the sound barrier with their three-wheeled creation. *Photograph courtesy Jane Van Aken.*

Bill Fredrick's rocket car races across the salt flat with driver Stan Barrett in one of many test runs held at varied locations. *Photograph courtesy Jane Van Aken.*

Opposite: Budweiser Rocket trio of Fredrick, Barrett and Needham during a media day promotion at Dodger Stadium. *Photograph courtesy Jane Van Aken.*

last 100 miles the most difficult. The one main technical problem is getting enough thrust to overcome the drag—the tradeoff of thrust versus drag. The car weighs 4,500 pounds with fuel, and the thrust is 12,000 pounds or higher. That's a very big push compared to the weight of the car. Keeping the car on the ground…is our big worry. If you stood the car on its back end and turned on the power, it would go straight up in the air."

Aerodynamicist Ray Van Aken contributed his highly regarded technical expertise to the rocket land-speed project. *Photograph courtesy Jane Van Aken.*

Van Aken describes Fredrick as "a self-taught apprentice in rocket-car research and application." It was Fredrick who designed the first rocket car, Courage of Australia, according to Van Aken.

"Fredrick has done a lot of work in the movies with rockets," said Van Aken. "In the films *Gator* and *Smokey and the Bandit*, he put together the rocket packages in which the cars flew great distances. The director of those two movies, Hal Needham, a former stuntman, became a driver for him."

Fredrick is also quite a promoter, says Van Aken. "He advertised in the *Los Angeles Times* for a woman driver for what was then called the SMI-Motivator, before Budweiser became a sponsor. He needed money, and the driver was asked to put up $20,000 for the right to drive. The women's land-speed record was just 302 miles per hour, and Fredrick knew it would do better than that. It was a way to instant fame. The calls that came in were very amusing. Most were from husbands, boyfriends and agents doing the speaking for the girls."

Stuntwoman Kitty O'Neil eventually went 512 miles per hour in the SMI-Motivator to shatter the women's land-speed record. Fredrick now has Barrett under contract for the unlimited land-speed record attempt.

"Kitty, as most people know, is deaf," said Van Aken. "She's a very courageous gal and understands that she got what she paid for. It's been a great career boost for her. This project has been as fascinating from the sidelines as much as anything."

In four days, on August 28, the main crew will arrive at the site east of Alturas to lay out and pack the course, get time systems verified, establish

The Rocket at the Smithsonian dedication ceremonies held on October 28, 1982, in Washington, D.C. *Photograph courtesy Jane Van Aken.*

fuel farms and implement telemetry and communications. On September 1, preliminary runs will begin, which will progress to firing tests and higher speeds until the historic speed-of-sound threshold is attained.

O'Neil and Needham tested the car at Bonneville, but the "salt was too hard and the car skipped," said Van Aken, adding that "if the car had rubber wheels instead of metal ones, it would have been okay."

The car had other difficulties at Mudd, near Tonopah, with Needham as driver. Alvord Lake was dropped as another site possibility because of environmental problems.

The Budweiser Rocket employs a three-stage fuel system. According to Van Aken, who is still finding science a fun experience after all these years, the final stage is the same solid propellant that was used for the Sidewinder guided missile, developed at China Lake.

Afterword: With an aid from its Sidewinder missile as a boost, the Budweiser Rocket was tracked at 739 miles per hour by U.S. Air Force personnel on

December 17, 1979, at Edwards AFB on the Rogers Dry Lake Bed (where space shuttles land) in being the first vehicle to break the speed of sound on land. Aerodynamics has been described simply as "the way air moves around things." The late 1920s saw the birth of the first rocket car. When Ray Van Aken describes Bill Fredrick as having "built the first rocket car," he might have focused on the type of liquid propellant used in making that distinction. O'Neil rode the rocket to glory in December 1976 at Alvord Dry Lake in Oregon and was immediately dubbed the "Fastest Woman on Earth." Fredrick was a math whiz in high school but, unlike the actual rocket scientists in abundance at China Lake, dropped out of UCLA after one year of engineering classes to support his family. The Motivator cost over $350,000 and had some thirty sponsors. Needham was originally targeted by Fredrick to pilot the Budweiser Rocket for a record run, but the nod ultimately went to Barrett.

Chapter 11

PEARSONVILLE DEMOLITION DERBY A REAL CRACKUP

Pearsonville, 1978

Demolition derby or destruction derby? Whichever you prefer, it's everything it's cracked up to be.

The cars are stripped of chrome, and the windows are removed for safety. After banging each other around in the manner of bumper cars at a carnival, the lone car still running is declared the winner. The poster advertising the third annual Turkey Classic at Pearson Speedway Sunday in Pearsonville describes the featured Destruction Derby with such phrases as "modern-day mayhem" and "controlled violence," whereupon "fearless daredevils smash each other at high speeds with the deliberate intention of crashing and wrecking each other…all in perfectly good cars."

That's plain enough.

Speedway entrepreneur Don Pearson calls it the "Battle of the Junkyards" because he has four cars in the derby, off the front line from his Speedway Auto Dismantling business in Pearsonville, and Tim Koch has four cars entered from his Sierra Auto Wrecking company in Ridgecrest.

Of the twenty or so entries, Lancaster's McPherson Auto Wrecking and Antelope Auto Wrecking are two of the out-of-town junkies bent on making a dent for derby honors.

In the past, Pearson has loaned some of his cars to drivers for a twenty-five-dollar fee with the stipulation that he gets them back afterward.

"Old cars are not easy to come by anymore," says Pearson. "If they're still capable of running, they're worth holding on to."

Pearson will try to control the mayhem in a '62 Lincoln. His '69 Chrysler was nosed out last year by Koch—well, Koch's car, because Koch himself crashed. "I got drunk," explained Koch. "I had to let a friend drive." The friend did a bang-up job. Not only did Sierra Auto Wrecking win the derby, but also Pearson, as second-place finisher, had to work a day at Koch's wrecking yard as per agreement. The bet is on again this year, and a confident Koch says he will win again. It's a sobering thought, but getting Pearson to work a day in his yard last year was no bargain. "He came in with a case of beer and some wine," said Koch. "He worked about an hour and drank the rest of the day."

Pearson admits he wasn't much help. "I went for the cutting torch the first thing," he said. "And that's a no-no. You don't cut parts off; you wrench them off. Then I told the first customer, 'We don't have that here. Why don't you try the Speedway?' He fired me."

Koch will go with a '70 white Chevy station wagon with "Doggie Daddy" slopped on its exterior in red paint. Out to win, he said the choice was not made at random. "I watched a high-roll destruction derby at the Los Angeles Coliseum on television in 1973," he said. "All the cars were brand-new. A Cad and Rolls were the first ones that stopped running, and a '73 Chevy station wagon won. Pearson's got a big Lincoln. I'll hammer him right in."

"He said that?" exclaimed Pearson when told of Koch's plan of destruction. "We're going to gang up on Tom right off anyway, so what he says doesn't matter."

"He's a good sport," countered Koch. "But a lot of people have great ideas that don't pan out."

Both Koch and Pearson have taken the precaution of placing their batteries on the front floorboard to ensure they won't get crushed. Koch has even gone a couple steps further. "I'm chaining my engine down so a knock won't slip the driveline from the back of the transmission." Additionally, he's removed the gas tank from the quarter panel and replaced it with a pony keg behind the front seat.

What does Pearson think of Koch's readiness? "That thing [the keg] will come loose and hit him in the back of the head, and then he won't think it's such a good idea."

Pearson is a veteran of five wreck-'em-ups, and Koch has participated in three. It is not the type of motorsport event one travels around the country to enter—unless one is a masochist at heart and has a number of moving scrap heaps to spare.

Koch, who prefers SCORE off-road races in his VW, offers his real strategy for winning a destruction derby: "You have to avoid getting hung up in a big pile. You have to keep moving. You stop, and you're like a lame duck. People are going to nail you."

Pearson, also an entrant in the Stock Car class thirty-lap main event on Sunday, has much the same philosophy: "Hit and run. Watch the front end. Keep your foot to the floor, and keep going."

Pearson organized his first destruction derby not at Pearsonville but at the rodeo grounds for the 1973 Desert Empire Fair held in Ridgecrest. He offered $150 in cash and a trophy for the main-event winner and $100, $50 and $25 prizes for runners-up. In the semi-main event, it was $75, $50 and $25. The top two women in the powder puff event received $50 and $25, respectively.

Afterword: Pearsonville was named for Andrew and Lucy Pearson and their wrecking yard, which they established in 1959 in eastern Kern County. For the Speedway's twenty-third annual Turkey Classic, held on Sunday, November 28, 1999, the nine-division event for Stock Cars paid a $16,000 purse. Sadly, that was near the end. The track, east on Pearson Road seven miles north of Star Route 14 on U.S. 395, closed following the 2000 season. In addition to the racetrack and junkyard, Pearsonville had a gas station and a trailer park. Popular events at the speedway were demolition derbies and figure-eight racing. The Turkey Classic was revived at the Route 66 Raceway in Victorville.

Chapter 12

COMEDIAN MAKES GOLF FUN AT STALLION SPRINGS

Tehachapi, July 1976

Stallion Springs' Horse Thief Country Club and Golf Course is sponsoring comedian Norm Crosby's first annual Hope for Hearing celebrity-amateur golf tournament. Ironic, perhaps, are the signs cueing motorists to "Keep Right," as the California Correctional Institution is visible where State Highway 202 ends. Creepy cult leader, convicted murder conspirator and former regional resident Charles Manson is not here, but a Mojave Desert acquaintance of his is: Robert "Ballarat Bob" Dunlap, who is in on a manslaughter conviction.

Tehachapi's rolling hills high up in the mountains are home to such Hollywood film stalwarts as Chuck Connors, Jack Palance and Noah Beery Jr. It's an old railroad town with the golf course about a dozen miles from downtown proper. Connors lives but a slice shot down the road, so says the driver of the forest-green shuttle bus that hauls visitors from the parking lot to the two-year-old golf course. "They are just regular folks," adds the driver, "…unless you get too personal."

As it turns out, none of the three are part of the celebrity group for the golf tournament.

Dozens of golf carts are aligned in military fashion as the shuttle flashes past a cluster of onlookers who quickly break up after eying this new shipment and deciding it contains not a single celebrity.

Inside the clubhouse, actor Dale Robertson offers up a handshake. He is easily recognizable from his television days as Jim Hardie, special investigator for Wells Fargo in the series *Tales of Wells Fargo*, and for his

Carpeteria floor covering television commercials. Born in Oklahoma, he lives in Los Angeles.

Appearing next is Crosby, the host of the tourney and the master of malapropisms, his comedy trademark.

Crosby is asked if he is a CBer, a participant in the current citizen-band radio craze some have dubbed the "Hula Hoop of the '70s."

"I don't have one, but I'm getting one," said Crosby, in what sounded like the start of one of his scrambled language skits. "But I am one," he said, finally answering the question. "I'm 'dictionary' to CB folks, and I love talking on the CB. I've flipped over it. We had one in our vehicle in Texas where I just finished playing the petroleum clubs and military bases."

He next glides into an impromptu routine: "You got a southbound looking for a northbound. See anything over your right shoulder? Yeah, a few hairs and some lint. But you should see under the arms. Sweatttty.

"Did you know those CB sets in Texas come with a drawl?" he continued. "I always thought Jantzen was a bathing suit until I landed in Landon B. Jantzen country."

Crosby himself has a hearing problem. This tournament he is hosting will provide funds earmarked for research programs at the University of California at Los Angeles. The Hope for Hearing Foundation was founded in 1959 by Edna Breslow.

In addition to Robertson, other celebs include Kenny Davis, a nightclub entertainer and leader of the Kenny Davis Trio, along with actor David Huddleston, memorable for his role in the movie *Blazing Saddles* and for starring with O.J. Simpson in *The Klansman*.

Oh, yes, there was some golf played. The banjo-plucking Davis and his group of R. Montgomery and Bob, Jeff and Pete Hildebrand won the golf tourney with an 11-under par 61.

Afterword: Crosby, born in 1927, served as a regular at Buck Owens's celebrity golf tourneys in Bakersfield, aimed at raising money for cancer research. He kept the links jokes coming when he published *Norm Crosby's Tee Party (The Official Golf Joke Book)*.

Chapter 13

YOUNG RIDER JOINS YAMAHA SUPPORT TEAM

Ridgecrest, October 25, 1978

I t is a sport for the young, motocross. That's just fine for Jeff Stanford, who at age fourteen is already a member of the Yamaha Motocross Support Team, a signal achievement for someone from the Indian Wells Valley region, where miles and miles of desert provide a nice practice track.

Stanford has just about reached his maximum in mini-cycles. Newly joined with the team, he was selected by the giant corporation as one of three 80cc Experts in Southern California.

Stanford receives two YZ80F motocross cycles and parts through 1979 and will ride prototype cycles as they become available for testing during the year. He and his father, Jim, picked up one of the production models last Friday at U.S. Yamaha in Buena Park.

Stanford's factory support selection is the first by a Ridgecrest motocross racer—not bad for someone who has been in the sport for barely two years.

"My first race was on August 14, 1976," informed Stanford. "I made it to the Grand Nationals in Ponca City, Oklahoma, held on August 11, 1978, less than two years later." He is not bragging; he's simply pointing out the near coincidence of the dates and taking pride in reaching the national level in less riding time than a lot of his competitors have been riding Expert.

Stanford has always set high goals for himself, such as the typed and signed, somber-toned oath tacked to a corkboard in the family kitchen, which reads:

> *I, Jeffery Charles Stanford, will always try at the best of my ability to race. I will not stop trying for any reason. My first goal is to beat Eric Kehoe,*

with him not falling or having any sort of trouble at all. My next goal is to be in the Race of Champions. If I get to be too big for the 80cc class, I will try to be a 125cc national champion. After that I will decide what I will do next. Those are my goals for now. February 23, 1978.

"Once he started writing his goals down, they started happening," said Jeff's mother, Eleanor.

"I'm about as far as I can go in minis now," he said, accepting a tray of just-baked and still-hot peanut butter cookies from his mother. "Being chosen for a support team is about as big an honor as you can get."

How about beating Eric Kehoe of Granada Hills?

"I've beaten him about four times," Jeff said. "He's fallen or done something crazy, but I've finished ahead of him. He's one of my biggest competitors. I've visited his home, and his dad has helped me with racing a lot of times. We're more friends than rivals. But on the track, we're all enemies."

Eleanor added, "People who participate in motocross, I've noticed, are friends in a family-type way. It kind of permeates the group."

"Right," said Jeff. "Nobody likes to see you at a disadvantage, so everyone helps out to see that everyone else has their bikes ready."

The mini-cycle class Stanford competes in includes peewee bikes, 50cc, 80cc and 100cc. The blond-haired "veteran" will soon outgrow the class and move to the 125cc class, but not until he hurdles a few more mini-cycle goals.

Stanford may someday reach the motocross heights of Bill Hannah, supported by Yamaha and supplied with a $100,000 250cc motorcycle. That is not on Stanford's current goal list. "I want to finish my goals on the wall first," he said. "I haven't made it to the Race of Champions yet."

To qualify for entry in the Race of Champions, a racer must be among the top in his region. Stanford challenges regularly in the World Mini Grand Prix at Trabuco Canyon. To win this fall series, he competes in five races every Sunday in October, with one winner selected according to a combined total point score for twelve-and-over riders in both stock and modified competition.

"I figure I'm fifth or sixth right now," said Stanford, not too enthused with his chances.

Most motocross tracks tend to be about one mile and a quarter in length, and like different golf courses, they have their own unique bends, twists, sharp turns, drop-offs, water and loose sand to deal with.

"In practice runs, you find out where the faster lines are, because when you're behind, you have to pass," noted Stanford. "When you decide to pass, you then have to beware of the other guys and their little tricks."

He said he has little time for other sports. "I do most of my concentrating on a motorcycle. After phys ed, I run home, play tennis in the street (his street is a cul-de-sac) and stay active. I don't lie around all week watching TV and then run on the weekends."

He describes the joys of the sport as "kind of a high when you win."

Afterword: Somewhere in the California desert near his Rancho Mirage home, Jeff can be found enjoying his new two-wheeler sport: road bicycle racing. After hitting the half-century mark in age, he has taken up a tamer machine. The days of wild abandon as a young teen are mostly history. Rarely did he practice at Sage Cycle Park in Ridgecrest in his younger days. Instead, he and like-minded friends left their back doors and shot across the open desert in their motorcycles, creating their own tracks and mastering every turn and maneuver imaginable. In 1979, he moved up to the 125cc class from 80cc and placed third in his very first intermediate race. Soon after, he traveled the country with his mom, Eleanor, as chaperon while racing a summer in the American Motorcyclist Association's exclusive Pro Class. Of the sixty or so competitors in that national circuit, he ranked in the top twenty. At his peak, he competed in as many as forty-two weekends during a calendar year, mostly out-of-town affairs with his dad, Jim. He was inspired to take up the sport by Ridgecrest motocross hero Rob Cosner.

Trabuco Canyon is a small community in Orange County near Rancho Santa Clarita. Sage Cycle Park drew much cycle news attention on February 23, 1975, when an estimated 2,500 persons showed up for a benefit motocross event. Competitors from all over Southern California raced, and local business provided food and lodging. Cliff Urseth, publisher of the *Daily Independent* newspaper, was one of the major sponsors.

Chapter 14

WHEN BASEBALL HAD REAL STARS

Ridgecrest, July 24, 1979

The Monogram Pictures Baseball Club, circa 1935, had Hollywood starlets and stars like Jimmy Cagney posing with the players for the team picture along with owner Trim Carr. Eugene McCormick, now sixty-six and a retired Ridgecrest businessman, was a star shortstop for the team while also working for the movie studio as a stagehand. After a semipro career on the field in baseball and softball, McCormick arrived in Ridgecrest in 1946 and forged a long relationship in the same sports as a coach.

McCormick played baseball for a team with real stars.

Movie stars like Jimmy Cagney, Ralph Bellamy and Edgar Kennedy and saucy starlets of the day did not actually play for the Monogram Pictures Baseball Club, but they were its supporting stars.

That was in the years 1934–36, long before Los Angeles Dodgers manager Tommy Lasorda had such clubhouse cronies as Frank Sinatra and Don Rickles.

McCormick, a former tire shop owner in Ridgecrest, even got a call—via telegram—to play a bit part in one of Monogram's college pictures, *Girl of My Dreams*, while working as a lot stagehand and playing baseball for the Sunday semipro studio team.

The telegram from Monogram's Lou Deutch read: "Report for work eight tomorrow morning…LA High School…wear clothes appropriate for attending college track meet…wear pants and sweater or something like that."

Several pro and semipro baseball players were on studio teams to play winter baseball. For example, Harry "Peanuts" Lowry, a St. Louis Cardinals outfielder of the 1950s, was on the Fox Studios nine when he was still a fuzz-cheeked youngster.

A real character, McCormick says, was one of his own teammates, Rosey Gilhousen, an ex-minor-league outfielder who is now a baseball scout living in Hawthorne, California. McCormick recalls, "Rosey was a strong stubby guy who said whatever was on his mind—even if they were shooting sound pictures. The directors would really get mad at him."

Some of the studio games were held at Sawtelle Field, which was a big treat for those who drifted over from the nearby old soldiers' home. "People would be sitting around doing their knitting," recalls McCormick. "A lot of them were sick and disabled, but when the game started, they put their knitting down and enjoyed the show."

McCormick was once a promising Major League baseball prospect. He graduated from Long Beach Poly High School in 1931, where he played every inning for four years as a shortstop/third baseman. In 1930, he was a member of Long Beach's first American Legion baseball team. At Compton Junior College, he teamed with his brother Eddie, a second baseman, to form a slick double-play combo. According to an old newspaper clipping, Eugene was described by his Compton coach as "the best leadoff hitter in the league, a nifty hitter and a sweet fielder." He was named to the all-time Compton team after graduating in 1935.

"I had a job at the time, and though I thought about signing with a professional club, I figured that I had gone to college to prepare myself for the working world, so I stayed where I was at," McCormick said.

McCormick had left Monogram for a full-time job with an engineering company. But he did not stop playing baseball and softball. In fact, he did not stop until he was forty-seven. He continued with semipro baseball and even got paid while with the Long Beach Nitehawks, softball world champions several times. The Nitehawks provided McCormick with some of his favorite recollections, especially when the irrepressible Lou Novikoff comes to mind. "He was nearly unbeatable," says McCormick, who has scrapbooks from his playing days with clippings as fresh as the morning newspaper. "Anytime he went out, you could just about count on a win. If he didn't pitch it, he'd get it with one over the fence."

Novikoff went on to star with the Chicago Cubs. "He gained so much weight in softball that he looked like a teddy bear with the Cubs," McCormick said of Novikoff.

Softball has not changed much, according to McCormick. "The class of that time with the class of today could go either way," he said. "They're not using slingshots or arrows. It's still manpower."

McCormick came to Ridgecrest in 1946 to open a tire business. The habit of sliding and bouncing back on his feet on the base paths left him with a bad hip and eventually ended his playing days. He remained active as a coach until a stroke partially limited his physical activities.

A big thrill for McCormick was helping Duke Martin coach the Indian Wells Valley Colt League team to a district championship in the late 1960s. With the advance, IWV lost to Brea and Randy Jones, now a star hurler for the San Diego Padres of the National League.

On the subject of the astronomical salaries players are receiving today, more power to the players, McCormick says. "I just wish they'd give me some of it," he joked. "Some fans really get upset when they find out what players are making. Not me. I say if they stick their hand out and someone wants to fill it, then they should take it. The progress is good—if they don't abuse it. They used to play in cow pastures, and it wasn't always a base they stepped on."

When asked which team he roots for today, McCormick said, "I used to pull for the Dodgers, but why should I pull for them now when they're not pulling for themselves? Why should I worry about them? I'd like to see the Cubs win it. They've had such a dry spell."

Afterword: Eugene Victor McCormick passed away in February 1985 at age seventy-two. His old team, the Los Angeles Nitehawks, was founded in 1933 and won ten world championships, the first one coming in 1953, years after McCormick played for them. The Nitehawks folded in 1988, ending a sterling chapter in the history of professional softball. Taft's Les Haney pitched for the Nitehawks and led the Taft Merchants to the World Softball Championship in 1948. Haney's pitching accomplishments were many, including his feat of averaging twenty-one strikeouts per game for forty-three consecutive games. Haney earned a nod in *Ripley's Believe It or Not!* when he allowed just two foul tips in striking out all twenty-seven batters he faced in a game in 1945.

Chapter 15

PRO RALLY RACING STARTED IN SUNDAY PARKING LOTS

Ridgecrest, March 16, 1979

Ray Hocker and co-driver Damon Trimble, in a 1978 Jeep CJ-7, challenged beefy GT models to place third in the 1978 NARRA series Unlimited Class. Not one to remain static, Hocker and new cockpit partner Tim Cox switched to the new Production Class with a Dodge Colt Lancer.

It's a side-street baby come of age, rally racing.

"Pro rallying developed from the Sunday sports car rally," says Hocker. "Those meetings in the parking lot that told you to go twenty-eight miles per hour and then turn at the third stoplight—that type of thing. When a group liked to drive fast, there were virtual races on American roads."

It wasn't long until clubs formed into national associations to serve as governing bodies for rally sports, the Sports Car Club of America (SCCA) having the largest following. Now, there's the North American Rally Racing Association (NARRA), a club Hocker helped found in 1976.

"NARRA was created because SCCA was not paying enough attention to rallying," informs Hocker, a husky twenty-four-year-old who, when his hands aren't on a steering wheel, usually has a Nikon in hand as a professional photographer. "SCCA holds two rally championships, and we have twelve. It's set up like the United States Auto Club, which rules all big-car racing. Points are earned at each race in the series, and the big one, the one where the money is, is the Pro Rally Championship."

Drivers go from transits, which may be the Holiday Inn parking lot in Hollywood, to stages, which may take them down Highway 101. Times are added for all stages, and the fastest time is the winner.

"Speeding on public roads is checked, and you can be heavily penalized," Hocker says. "Also, the events are public knowledge, and a state trooper may catch you coming down a hill and take you to jail."

John Buffum, from Vermont, is the current NARRA champion. Hocker finished third behind Hendrik Blok. Any legally licensed vehicle can run, from pickups to Porsche Carreras. The four top cars last year, however, were GTs.

"A guy could have it wrapped up in five events," Hocker notes. "But as it worked out last year, four or five traded back and forth all year." Hocker, with co-driver and half brother Damon Trimble, created somewhat of a stir among the GT crowd with his American Motors Jeep CJ-7.

"We were the only privateer," said Hocker, which means the team did not have a full sponsor. "We were new, and everywhere we went, they'd whisper, 'Who are they?' That was at first. Later, they worried about us, especially if it was raining. We're not a swift GT car. What we lack in speed we make up in durability and traction in snow and muddy spots."

Hocker and Trimble weaved through sugarcane fields and mushed across dark rain forests to win the 1978 Las 24 Horas de Puerto Rico unlimited class, a twenty-four-hour race and the second largest in that country. Trimble, a thirty-four-year-old IBM executive based in Newark, California, and a former jet pilot, has signed to drive with Blok's Chrysler team this year.

"There's no hard feelings," Hocker notes. "I used to race with Chrysler. It's better for him. There'll be no money out of his pocket, and he'll be going to England, South America and around the country in a very competitive car."

Getting the jeep ready for the first SCCA series run at the end of this month is one of Hocker's present concerns, along with the ever-present hunt for sponsors. Plus, he'll need a new co-driver.

"The co-driver is very important in staging," Hocker says. "He tells you in advance where to turn from the route book and gives you only the information you want to know. It's a very direct communication. The co-driver is also the on-board bookkeeper. He turns scores in at check points to show how you're doing."

And Hocker's not doing bad for a Sunday driver in a Jeep.

HOCKER TRIES A DIFFERENT CLASS

June 7, 1979

Last year, Hocker's 1978 CJ-7 Jeep proved that a four-wheel-drive vehicle can be competition for the sleek, sports-type rally cars. Hocker pushed the Jeep to the third highest points total in the North American Rally Racing Association.

Now Hocker has made a switch. He has chosen to compete in the newly formed NARRA Production Class, the rules of which limit engine modification. Hocker and co-driver Tim Cox are driving a new Dodge Colt Lancer, similar to the one that won the famous East African Safari Rally.

"It has to be darn near showroom stock," says Hocker of cars in the Production Class. "You can do things to make it a little more survivable, but nothing to boost performance."

Knowing that some people will joke about it once the word "Polish" comes up, Hocker usually starts off talking about his survival accessories by saying, "I'm one of the few drivers, if not the only one, who uses Polish driving lights." After the usual laughs he gets, he adds, "But they're good. They're Zelmot SL-500 Delta Beams. A company called Durimex markets the lights, and they came to us. They're young like our team, and we're both out to beat the big guns and the big bucks."

And once again, Hocker, twenty-four, will be rallying on Uniroyal tires. Uniroyal selected their Rallye 240 tires for the Colt team.

But the question remains: why did Hocker leave the Unlimited Class for the Production Class?

"It's kind of an ego boost to do well in stock against the unlimited cars," he said. "We [NARRA] started the stock class last year as a trial. As a matter of fact, Mike Gibeault from Ridgecrest was the champion. It was a test to see how it would work—kind of a poor man's class with low bucks. Basically, the car you compete in, you can drive back and forth to work."

Hocker said the added Production Class worked very well in California, which prompted NARRA to sanction it nationally. "I think it's going to be a real boon to the sport, a new challenge," he said. "People can come out now without having to put thousands of dollars in their engines. Unlimited cars have up to $20,000 invested. I can compare it with the International Race of Champions, where twenty drivers, all in Camaros, draw numbers and find out who is the best driver."

Another example Hocker likes to use is that of Mark Donohue, a driver who once made winning Can-Ams a habit—too much of a habit, some say.

"He was putting more money into it than anyone else," said Hocker. "His equipment was vastly superior. It became the same in rally racing. Four or five cars were always great, but if you didn't have $15,000, you couldn't compete with them."

After two races this year, the Olympus in Olympia, Washington, and the Mendocino Forest Rally in Willows, California, Hocker figures he is somewhere in the top five in Production Class. "I think we can win the stock class, and overall, we're shooting for the top ten," said Hocker, a privateer in the rally circuit battling, for the most part, factory teams.

It may be a little ironic that Hocker's Jeep, pictured recently in *Popular Mechanics* magazine, could have served him well at the Olympus. No one laughed at the box-shaped rally machine when it was raining and muddy. Hocker's Colt stuck in the mud in Washington, and that may have cost him a win. But the Jeep is gone, and Hocker has found a new challenge.

Racing automobiles may be a glamour sport in some areas, but Hocker says rally racing is not the best thing for the old ego: "Not when you've got your car upside down…it's a real deflator. You're out there alone, and nobody sees it."

Hocker and Cox, who handles the countdowns as co-driver, will be flying in their yellow Colt, perhaps less alone than before in the new, rising class.

Afterword: Bill Moore was Hocker's navigator for several 1979 rallies. It worked out well for Blok/Trimble. Later in the year, they captured the 1979 NARRA championship in their Plymouth Arrow entry. The two had teamed the previous December to win a rally in California City. Hocker himself was a co-driver for Ron Richardson in 1977 when they won the championship, also in a Plymouth Arrow. Though a highly regarded driver, Hocker might be best remembered as an organizer and innovator. In 1976, Hocker was the inaugural organizer for the Rim of the World Championship held in Palmdale. The Jeep CJ-7 was a favorite for mud racing and rock crawling.

Chapter 16

1972: GOLDEN YEAR FOR BURROUGHS HIGH BASEBALL

Ridgecrest, May 30, 1979

The 1972 Golden League baseball all-league team was one they still talk about. Burroughs High had three seniors on the elite roster: Steve Robinson, Mark Wooten and Jerry Mather. Of the three, only Robinson advanced to the professional level, in the Philadelphia Phillies farm chain. Freshman Amos Blanche was an honorable mention selection.

The Burros were 10–4 on the year and wound up in a second-place GL tie. Some of the other league names from that year may be more familiar.

Wooten, who batted .350, narrowly edged out Antelope Valley's Dwayne Murphy for a first-team outfield spot. Murphy is now a fledgling fly chaser for the Oakland A's. Murphy hit .376 in settling for a second-team GL nod.

Making the squad as a utility man was Jason Thompson, a .356 belter for Apple Valley, who is now a supernova playing the initial position for the Detroit Tigers.

Apple Valley first baseman Rick Ollar led the league with a .442 batting average and was rightly recognized as the player of the year. Ollar signed with the Los Angeles Dodgers but faded away after a few minor-league summers, including a stop in Bakersfield.

That brings us to Robinson and his baseball odyssey. For the six-foot-two, two-hundred-pounder, his all-league selection in '72 was the second consecutive time he was named the league's premier third baseman. He was impressive on the mound as well, but the top pitcher for the Burros was Mather.

Mather, in ninety-seven innings, was 7–0 with a 1.79 ERA. Robinson averaged nearly two strikeouts per inning but was used sparingly.

Manager George Ridgley must have deemed third base best for Robinson. Robinson, now twenty-five, is a junior majoring in physical education at San Diego State.

"A lot of scouts called me and asked when I was going to pitch," he recalled. "What could I tell them?"

But come signing time, the Phillies remembered. Robinson was a versatile prospect, and the team signed him to a free-agent contract. It was about the time rookie camps were opening, and Robinson was assigned to one in Pulaski, Virginia. He was in shape upon arriving, thanks to having played American Legion baseball for Quartz Hill on the weekends and traveling to Bakersfield twice a week for Kern County League games.

Robinson's first real season was in 1973 at Spartanburg, South Carolina, in the Class A Western Carolinas League, where he posted a 13–9 record, second best in the league, to go with a 2.86 ERA, 140 strikeouts and just 39 walks in 195 innings. His 13 wins surpassed future Major Leaguers John Candelaria, Frank LaCorte and Preston Hanna.

A major highlight for Robinson came when he broke an eleven-year-old Western Carolinas League record while pitching for the Spartanburg Phillies on August 21, 1973. The nineteen-year-old pitched a four-hitter to run his record to 12–9 overall, but in winning nine of his last twelve decisions, he had also gone twenty-eight innings without yielding a base on balls. The previous record of consecutive innings pitched without a walk was twenty-four. "It was a good year," Robinson said. "We were dead last the first half and came back to win the league title."

Robinson was not promoted for his efforts.

When the season opened in 1974 for Rocky Mount (North Carolina) in the Carolinas League, Robinson was still in Class A. "All of a sudden, they wanted to make me into a reliever," he said. "They said it was because I had good control and it was an easier way to the Majors. Since I was a free agent and they had no big money wrapped up in me, if I'd said no, it would have been, 'See ya, kid.'"

Robinson was doing fine in his new role until a sinker—a reliever's staple he added to his standard starter's repertoire of fast ball, curve, slider and change—prompted an elbow injury to his throwing arm. "One pitch did it," he said. "A Rocky Mount doctor examined me and said the muscle damage would take six weeks of rest to cure. But the Phillies flew me to Philadelphia, and the team doctor there said I should work with weights and throw regularly on the sidelines. The doctor, Phillip Marone, said it was just a slight injury. I thought it a little weird that two doctors would have two entirely different opinions. I threw on the sidelines for three quarters of the season and worked with weights. The elbow never did heal right."

Robinson came back in 1975—in somewhat of a surprise visit, he said—but the arm was not healed, and it was just a matter of time before the axe fell in the form of his release. "I came for spring training and felt a lot of strange vibes. It was like, 'Oh, you're with us again.' I felt like I'd proven in '73 that I was better than Class A. Before the arm trouble, my manager told me my stuff was good enough for the Majors. That was when they sent me to Rocky Mount for long relief."

Robinson did get in seventy-six innings with three saves before receiving his walking papers. "They said I wasn't a prospect any longer," he recalled. "I was pretty disappointed. At least I felt good knowing I was on two league-championship teams in my four years."

Robinson married a Ridgecrest girl, and the two have lived in San Diego the past two years. Knowing that you cannot live baseball forever, he harbors no regrets about his aborted fling to reach the big time. "That's life," he said.

However, he did pursue the answer to one question. "In 1976, I decided to go the [Los Angeles] Rams' doctor and find out if this elbow thing was real or just in my head. They took extensive X-rays and found that the muscles were indeed torn away and that since I had aggravated them, they hadn't grown back right. By this time, there was no need for an operation, so I just took some pills for awhile at the doctor's suggestion."

It may be a cliché, but for every Jason Thompson and Dwayne Murphy, there really are hundreds like Steve Robinson with similar stories to tell. But why dwell on what might have been? That 1972 group stands alone as a grand memory.

MARTIN FIRST MAJOR LEAGUER FROM RIDGECREST

When J.D. (John Dale) Martin stepped on the mound for the Washington Nationals against the New York Mets on July 20, 2009, the Ridgecrest-born pitcher became the first from his hometown to play Major League baseball. Martin was born in Ridgecrest on January 2, 1983. His older brother, Kevin, was a pitcher who spent four years in the minors with the Indians (2001–04). J.D. spent several years in the minors before his call-up. John Martin, father of J.D. and Kevin, pitched in the minors as a Yankees and Angels farmhand (1968–69). John's first season in 1968 was with Johnson City (Tennessee).

That was the same minor-league Yankees team that Ridgecrest's Tommy Mather pitched for in his lone 1967 pro season.

Another Ridgecrest baseball connection, Joe Norris, was born in Lone Pine in Inyo County in 1970. Norris graduated from Burroughs High in 1988, was drafted by the Montreal Expos from Bakersfield College in 1989 and pitched nine years in the minor leagues (1990–98). Minor-league rosters listed him as residing in Inyokern. Although he was never a Major League player, he was traded for one. In 1993, the Expos traded Norris to the Minnesota Twins organization for outfielder Derek Lee, who had played in fifteen Major League games for the Twins in a one-month period in 1993.

Afterword: Amos Blanche was drafted by the Oakland A's in 1979 while attending Antelope Valley Junior College. He played briefly for the Medford (Oregon) A's in 1980.

Part II
WESTERN KERN COUNTY

Chapter 17
MATMEN READY TO CRUSH ALL COMERS

Bakersfield, November 1975

Since monies for so-called marginal athletics (those with nominal dollar potential) are virtually nonexistent for many of the colleges involved in today's mad sports whirl, the fact that Cal State Bakersfield has a wrestling program is no small miracle. It is even more impressive when you consider that last year, CSB's matmen were rated among the country's best. While Coach Joe Seay (pronounced SEE) has yet to take his first walk across Kern River, he has performed the "Miracle at Stockdale Highway," with a fourth-season premier set for November 19 at Fullerton.

Colleges are forced by economics and ramifications of Title IX (gender equity) to think small. From a financial standpoint, that means sports like volleyball, handball, tennis and, if you are really pinched, croquet. Mostly, it amounts to no more than token calisthenics. Nobody told Seay that his chances of gaining national recognition with such a splintered program were merely a bad joke.

"Never have so few gone so far on so little" might serve as the inspirational motto for the C-Men. At times using makeshift equipment and inconvenient off-campus training shuttles, Seay's crew has finished third, second and first in three years of league standings. Last year, four of his charges placed nationally; in league finals, CSB captured every weight event—all this in under less-than-optimum conditions.

"We've all been like a bunch of gypsies in the different athletic departments," said Seay during a Sunday phone interview. "It's great to have

Cal State Bakersfield wrestling coach Joe Seay set the standard for all Roadrunner sports teams. *Photograph courtesy of* Bakersfield Californian.

a place to practice where we have clean equipment and proper facilities." Seay, of course, was referring to the new gym.

Last year, CSB was rated third in the college division. Divisions are designated according to the number of sports the school supports. Division I is made up mostly of universities, hence the "university" designation. Division II is the "college" division, where coffers are not quite as abundant as they are in DI, and Division III is composed of schools with little financial backing to support sports. The divisions are an attempt to establish a system to rate competition fairly.

Is CSB capable of successfully meeting Division I competition? "About 70 percent of our schedule is with Class I schools," Seay reported. "We have a tougher schedule this year than last. I like it that way because it brings out our best, and I want the people to see the best wrestling there is."

Seay said he would not be bashful against taking on DI schools such as Oklahoma State, a team with twenty-seven national titles. He's even looking forward to dueling UCLA. "Last year, we were 16–4 in dual meets after losing our first one to UCLA, and this has probably been their best recruiting year ever. They had a good team before they recruited." The enthusiasm was apparent in his voice when he mentioned the Westwood Boulevard gang.

Does Seay ever feel like entering the arena with his own grapplers and engaging in a good-natured tussle? "I do. That's the way I coach. I'm very competitive with my wrestlers, and I'm glad that I'm still young enough…I don't know what I'll do when I get too old," he laughed.

The addition of Bill Van Worth, a local product fresh from picking up a gold medal, and assistant coach Dan Mello (both participants in the Pan American Games at Mexico City) helps renew the momentum of last year's league clincher. Van Worth, a 290-pounder, redshirted last year as a Humboldt State transfer.

The Pan-Am style of wrestling is Greco-Roman—a form emphasizing a "hands off" policy below the waist. While CSB is regulated more by the rules of "freestyle" wrestling, Seay feels Van Worth and Mello's proficiency in the Greco-Roman style will help squad workouts. Seay, a Kansas State mat standout and Greco-Roman stylist, said, "Dan, at 126, can work with the lower-weight wrestlers in upper-body techniques. I'm about 160 and can work intermediate and up, and Bill can take on the heavies."

How about using sheer strength to get the other guy to holler uncle? "A strong man will not get very far without technique, and there are several techniques one must learn," said Seay.

The style for men in recent years has gone to longer hair—a style embraced by Seay and some of his wrestlers. Is this not an unnecessary detriment? "There are guidelines," said Seay. "I think the rules try to abide with the times. For instance, hair on the sides is supposed to fall near the middle of the ear and in the back, not beyond the collar. Personally, I'm not interested in all that. What I care about is attitude—attitude toward class and practice. I'm interested in the person. I don't care about hair unless it gets in the eyes. Being well groomed is the main thing, and there is no question that some men look better with long hair."

When asked to name the single most effective wheelhorse on the squad, Seay said, "I'd say about all of them."

Actually, the roster reads more like a "Who's Who Among College Wrestlers." It is a formidable list, and helping direct it is Bill Kalivas, a graduate assistant from last year's team.

Are wrestlers superstitious? Or does their intense concentration deprive them of this oddity among athletes? "Sure," said Seay. "It's human nature, I think. I know I've got men who put on their left shoe last…things like that. That's in all sports."

So, with all their achievements, they are still human after all.

Seay stresses the educational part of college as the most important, pointing out that wrestling has not yet opened up to the big-money game. Volleyball and tennis have formed recent pro leagues, but not wrestling.

"A heavyweight such as Van Worth can usually fare well in professional acrobatics—or acting," as Seay refers to the professional wrestling circuit. "Is there any doubt it is acting?" Seay asks rhetorically.

Seay coached wrestling for eight highly successful years at South High before coming to CSB in 1972. At home, the fourth-year Roadrunner coach has a squad worth mentioning: his wife, Sue, and three daughters—Jody, Julie and Jill.

Born in Altus, Oklahoma, in 1939, Seay attended school in Wellington, Kansas, and wrestled collegiately for Kansas State, where he earned his master's degree in 1964. He was a three-time Greco-Roman national champion and twice was runner-up. He finished second in the 1964 and 1972 Greco Olympic trials and was third in the freestyle trials in 1968. He often has fanatic (although small) crowds at CSB. To help bolster attendance, he invited the Roadrunner cheerleaders to lend support.

The cheerleaders knew little about wrestling.

"One of the girls kept screaming, 'Grab his leg, grab his leg!'" recalled Seay. "Finally, I couldn't take it any longer, and I had to turn and quietly tell her, 'If that's all you know about wrestling, don't say anything at all.'"

Afterword: Seay, a Bakersfield resident for twenty years, left CSB in 1984 for Stillwater and the Oklahoma State Cowboys. At CSB, he spent twelve years developing the nation's most powerful NCAA Division II wrestling program. At Bakersfield, Seay won over 77 percent of his matches in compiling a 189–56–2 record, especially impressive considering the Roadrunners competed against both Division I and Division II teams. He led his squad to seven Division II national titles, including four in his last five years. Seay is the only coach to be named Coach of the Year in both Division II and Division I. He was also national high school coach of the year while at South High in Bakersfield. He was the U.S. Olympic head coach in 1996 for the gold medal–winning team. His achievements and those of his wrestlers are many and impressive.

WRESTLING PROGRAM SAVED FROM ELIMINATION

An announcement came in 2010 with bad news. The college's wrestling program, now a Division I competitor in the Pac-10, would be eliminated due to budget restraints. On Saturday night, February 13, 2010, in a final home match, team members wore black sweats and singlets with no lettering or logos as a form of expression regarding the elimination of their sport. The golf and tennis programs were also dropped. About $2 million was needed to keep the programs afloat for an undetermined amount of time. T.J. Kerr, the coach for the past twenty-five years, stepped down to sacrifice his salary. Stephen Neal, a right guard for the New England Patriots and a former two-time national wrestling champion for the Roadrunners, was a big help in raising money to keep the programs active. Kerr, who led the wrestlers to two Pac-10 championships (1996, 1999), died on June 5, 2013, at age sixty-four. He was replaced by Mike Mendoza.

Chapter 18
TEAM ROPERS WATKINS AND MORENO

Taft, April 28, 1978

D ennis Watkins's full-time baptism into professional rodeo team roping began in June 1974. The blond, twenty-two-year-old Taft native made it all the way to the national finals that year (even after a midyear start), and he has continued that tradition every year since, including his national television appearance in Oklahoma City last year.

"The top fifteen money winners for the year qualify for the finals," informed Watkins, who earned $8,648 and finished twelfth in team roping for the Professional Rodeo Cowboys Association in 1977. Adding to his regular-season winnings, Watkins teamed with steady partner Julio Moreno of Bakersfield, whom he's known since age ten, at the nineteenth PRCA National Finals in Oklahoma City last December and split $4,068 to run his year's total to $10,682.

On the PRCA circuit, each dollar represents a point earned.

Watkins and Moreno won the opening go in the finals with a 6.8-second time, placed fourth in another round and finished third overall. The two finished sixth in 1976.

Moreno finished eleventh during the regular season with $8,797 in earnings, and counting his winnings in the finals, he ended the year with $10,831.

The two split points evenly; therefore, the difference in totals lies in the fact that "Julio went to a rodeo that I didn't want to go to," explained Watkins. "He got another partner and finished in the money."

Watkins figures he and Moreno are ranked about eleventh or twelfth in the current standings, which is a better start than he had at this time last year.

In explaining their roles, Watkins said, "Moreno always heads, and I always heel. He's the quarterback. He sets up the play, and I finish it out."

1977 NATIONAL FINALS RODEO OKLAHOMA CITY
©FAIN PHOTOGRAPHIC, LTD.

Team roper Dennis Watkins loses his cowboy hat in action at the 1977 National Finals Rodeo held in Oklahoma City with partner Julio Moreno. *Photograph courtesy Dennis Watkins.*

As the header, Moreno ropes the steer's horns, being careful not to hit the rope barrier, and Watkins loops around the back legs in his role as heeler. Once around the legs, Watkins jerks the slack and "dallies" the rope around his saddle horn. Both ropes have to be tight, the steer stretched out in the middle and the two horses facing each other to finalize the event.

"Any kind of a 7-second run will usually get you a check," said Watkins. "Once, I took fourth with a 6.1, but that doesn't happen very often. Between 7 and 7.5 is a good run."

If Watkins ropes only one foot, he has to suffer a five-second penalty. And if Moreno gets out too fast and breaks the rope barrier string, ten seconds is added on. "You can lose fingers in the dally," said Watkins. "A lot of people have. I've come close. But when you rope together as much as Julio and I have, that rope becomes a part of you. Still, I guess I've been lucky."

Watkins's best year was in 1976, when he finished "eighth or ninth" for the year. The difference in that year and last year's twelfth place amounts to about $2,600, he says.

Cathy, a Chowchilla girl who became Watkins's bride in January, "takes care of the horses and drives a lot."

"I'm going to take Super 8 movies of Dennis to study," she said. "I've taken some, but we plan to make it a regular thing."

When he's at home, Watkins practices in his father Eddie's arena in Valley Acres. Eddie, by the way, has an RCA card and performs part time.

"A man's only human," Watkins says regarding practice. "You can't get it down to where you'll never miss. It's a sport that can be broken down scientifically in its methods, but it's the only individual sport left in the United States."

Watkins estimates covering up to seventy thousand miles per year in traveling to rodeo meets. "I travel by motor home when Cathy and I go together," he said. "That saves motel and food expenses. Other times, I drive a pickup and camper and take along a couple of buddies to split expenses."

When an event comes up that Watkins wants to enter, he calls Rocom, a computer in Denver that can be reached by toll-free number, and gives his and Moreno's name, event and desired entry place. "The computer then gives a 'call back' time for two or three days later so that we can find out when we're up," he explained. "That way, they close their entry books fairly early, and when we get there, we pay the rodeo secretary."

The two ropers keep in touch often by telephone. There are, however, no sick calls. "If we're sick, we go anyway," said Watkins. "I was out six weeks in 1976 with torn ligaments in one of my knees, and Julio had to find another partner. Hurt yes, sick no."

Watkins and Moreno pay their own travel expenses and are charged an entry fee even before they can take their turn for the money.

"We make it by what we win," said Watkins. "One go-round usually costs $30. Two go-rounds can be $75 to $100. At the Denver National Western Stock Show, it's $200 for two go-rounds. The total time on both steers wins there."

A team roper hardly ever strays farther east than Kansas, Oklahoma or Minnesota, adds Watkins. "It hasn't really caught on back east, but it will."

Pretty soon, Watkins will be adding up plenty of IRS tax deductions.

"From June until the end of August, we'll be roping hard," he said. "You get what they call 'White Line Fever.' I make about seventy-two rodeos a year."

Watkins, who also does some calf roping during the season, says that at five-foot-six and 150 pounds, he's "a little small." The average roper, he figures, is around five-foot-nine and 170 pounds. "To keep in shape," Watkins adds, "you need to run a little bit. And you should ride your horse every day because the horse has to stay in good shape, too." He and Cathy say Banner, their horse, is considered one of the best heeling horses in the business.

Afterword: Watkins resides in Bakersfield with his wife, Cathy, a schoolteacher. In recent years, he has teamed mainly with David Motes, and the two have earned more than $500,000 in prize money.

Chapter 19
SKYDIVERS SEARCHING FOR MORE OF THE SKY

Taft, July 17, 1978

Ron Shipe is a thirty-one-year-old Taft machinist and coordinator for a parachute demonstration team that likes nothing better than floating around heaven all day. When he comes down to earth, however, the choice of landing spots is not as unlimited as those assortments of cloud calisthenics performed in the blue.

Landing on or near the target, called the drop zone (DZ), a huge circle of plowed earth is also part of the sport, in addition to the air stunts.

Shipe contends that detractors of the sport are responsible for it not getting the recognition and respect it deserves in Kern County and especially in Taft, where jumpers use a DZ situated on a land parcel they call "The Ranch," located within some two hundred acres east of the aqueduct on property owned by Art Armstrong, one of the pioneers of skydiving here.

"We're a commercial outfit, not a club," Shipe clarified. "We have an exhibition team of about twenty members called the West Coast Pelican Skydivers. Our primary interest is in getting a drop zone at the [Taft] airport." The county airport at Taft, where Hangar No. 1 houses a licensed rigger loft for Art Armstrong's Taft School of Sport Parachuting, is a tenant of Standard Oil of California.

"We also want to do water jumps at Buena Vista and maybe a jump at the Elks Rodeo on Father's Day. But we can't get anywhere," Shipe said. "We can't seem to get any jumps in Kern County. They're afraid of the liability. If we didn't have a drop site on Art's property, we wouldn't have one, period. The drop zone used to be on navy property, but the college has an agricultural thing there now."

Shipe admitted that jumpers had actually landed on the roofs of some Taft homes when the drop site had been at its old location closer to town. "That wouldn't be a problem again," he said. "Only those qualified to jump in town [at the airport] would be allowed to make jumps."

Shipe carries a card issued to him by the California Department of Transportation that authorizes, or "qualifies," him to make exhibition jumps.

There are no female members among the Pelicans, but Becky Shipe, Ron's wife, who makes trips from the airport to town and back for refreshments when the team is jumping, says Standard Oil is blocking attempts by the skydivers to move the DZ to the airport. "Standard Oil has something against skydivers," she said. "We haven't found out what it is. The county seemed to be going along with us, and then all of a sudden, they backed out."

Becky said that since the members are covered, liability should not be a factor. "If you don't have liability insurance to cover you, then you have to join the United States Parachute Association, where a twenty-dollar fee will cover the possibility of you landing on a car or something. We also have a waiver," she said.

Ray Hicks, land department head in Taft for Chevron USA, the brand name used by Standard Oil of California, denies that Standard has acted as a villain against the skydivers in their attempts to relocate a drop zone at the airport or in denying them exhibition jump privileges in general. Hicks said:

> We talked to a lot of people about locating the drop zone at the airport. We found nobody for it except the skydivers. That included pilots, who were dead set against it, and our tenant, Kern County. Our attorneys said the insurance waiver was not sufficient. County attorneys also pointed out that the waiver was not broad enough. Our attorneys told us not to stick our necks out.
>
> If I told you everyone who was against it, it would be embarrassing. Our attorney's opinions are the only thing we can hang a hat on. We're not asking them to get more protection. It's a nuisance sport that we don't want. It's a dangerous sport with a lot of deaths in it. There's also a special vulnerability involving third-party claims. The risk involved to Standard and its tenant just isn't worth the risk. It's easy to sue us, and people like to sue big companies. We tried very hard to justify it. I hope they continue. I asked them to use the navy land. Landing in a bull's-eye is one thing, but coming down in power lines and on people's roofs is another.

Ron Shipe disagrees. With defined boundaries, he feels skydiving is not the dangerous sport some people believe it to be—nor does he understand how other areas honor the waiver and allow jumps while Kern County denies it.

"The waiver has been proven time and time again throughout the country," Shipe said. "Still, they say it's no good. We paid a lawyer seventy-five dollars to study it, and he said it was okay. We don't believe the county actually checked it out. We don't think they went that far."

Shipe said he moved to Taft from Santa Barbara five years ago because the latter would allow exhibition jumps but not a permanent drop zone. He felt it would be different here. He's such an enthusiast of the sport that he once made a jump while wearing a back brace sustained from a previous jump injury.

And indeed, the Pelicans do seem to keep busy in other parts of California. "Last August, the air show committee at Paso Robles picked our team over the Golden Knights, the U.S. Army team. We'll be back this year," Shipe said. "At the county fair in San Luis Obispo, CBS filmed us, and it was on nationwide television."

The group's most recent exhibition was in participation with the Fourth of July fireworks show held at Pierce College in Woodland Hills. More than half of the Pelicans are from the Los Angeles area. "We didn't make any money out of it," said Shipe. "In fact, the most money I've ever seen a jumper get for one jump is twenty dollars. We don't make much money, but we enjoy it."

At Pierce College, the Pelicans performed a stunt that must have looked good to the fireworks crowd on the ground. Two helicopters gave off a trail of yellow smoke to start the jump run and then went to 10,500 feet so the team could prepare for the snowflake formation. Four jumpers from one copter bailed out and formed a star, while the four from the other aircraft each grabbed a leg on the snowflake. Each jumper had "smoke"—an army surplus smoke grenade fastened on a special boot bracket—on one leg. The jumpers pulled the ring while on the runners of the helicopters. At 5,500 feet, those holding on to a leg let go and trailed off. The first four then went into a spin for several revolutions. At 2,000 feet, canopies opened.

"A lot of people come up here to jump from Los Angeles," said Shipe. "It gets too crowded down there because there are so many. I just wish we could get something going here—anything."

But with Standard's firmly opposed attitude—and the county siding with the company—the skydivers are up against mighty odds.

Afterword: On October 17, 1982, a Twin Beech airplane carrying eleven skydivers, one jumpmaster and one observer left the Taft airport and, soon after takeoff, dropped from 150 feet (on a target climb of 12,500 feet) and crashed nose down on the ground, killing all occupants. Monty "Spike" Yarter, a one-eyed pilot from Los Angeles with a solid flying reputation, was the oldest aboard, at age sixty-five. James Sword, a twenty-two-year-old from Bakersfield, and Etoula Van Pelt, a thirty-eight-year-old from Lost Hills, were the Kern County casualties. The majority of the passengers resided in the Los Angeles region. Van Pelt's husband, Norman, was manager of the Taft parachuting school. When the couple married, they performed the ceremony in the air. Some of those who perished performed for the West Coast Pelicans. The plane had been used the weekend before for stunts in the TV series *The Fall Guy*. The tragedy was a near repeat of history. On October 14, 1962, a pilot and thirteen skydivers aboard an airplane over a parachute drop zone were all killed as the plane stalled and crashed. The crash occurred eight miles southeast of Taft at a strip operated by Art Armstrong's Taft School of Sport Parachuting. Federal investigators determined that the plane was overloaded.

Chapter 20
BICYCLIST RECALLS 1936 BERLIN OLYMPICS

Bakersfield, March 1980

Charles Morton, a sixty-four-year-old Bakersfield resident and former Olympian, soft-pedals any talk of boycotting the 1980 Summer Olympic Games in Moscow.

A member of the five-man road cycling team in the famed 1936 Berlin Olympics, Morton offers this parallel: "We had much the same situation then. Hitler was going all over Europe doing his dirty work. We still had the games, and we came out okay."

History reveals that a great debate existed in America over whether the United States should participate in the eleventh Olympics in Berlin because of the Nazi Party. Finally, Avery Brundage, then president of the U.S. Olympic Committee, opined that the plight of Jews in Germany was of no concern to the sports world.

"Germany won the Olympics that year," Morton reminded, adding with an ironic smile that "the big joke was that they gave themselves gold medals for floral design. How else could they have won it? We had so many places it was pathetic."

German chancellor Adolf Hitler looked upon the games as an opportunity to showcase Nazism. But the star of the show turned out to be Jesse Owens, a black, liquid-smooth athlete who once broke world records in the one-hundred- and two-hundred-yard dashes and broad jump and tied the two-hundred-meter hurdles mark—all within an hour—for Ohio State in a Big Ten Conference meet.

Owens's prowess on the track in Berlin was equally remarkable. It was enough to send Hitler's Aryan race supremacy propaganda clicking back on its heels and cause "der führer" to become "the furious."

"I was there the day Hitler got up and walked out when the flags went up for Owens," Morton said. "We didn't know then why he left, but you should have heard the talk in the village that night. Jess? He just laughed about it."

Owens could afford a laugh or two. He was the only track-and-field performer to win more than one gold medal in Berlin (he earned four), setting world records in the one-hundred-yard dash and the broad jump, winning the two-hundred-yard dash and anchoring the winning four-hundred-yard relay.

The boycott topic initiated by President Jimmy Carter concerns sending Moscow our regards but not our athletes this summer, due to government-described invasions of Afghanistan by Soviet troops.

"Sure, I think the Russians are off-kilter, but the games shouldn't be stopped for political reasons," Morton said. "A lot of the kids have trained hard, and some won't get a second chance. Age is especially crucial in sports such as cycling."

Morton estimates the best age for cyclists at somewhere between twenty-one and twenty-seven. Morton was twenty when he finished nineteenth in his one and only Olympics. The old man of the '36 cycling team was New Jersey's John Sinabaldi, twenty-seven, a repeater from the 1932 Olympics.

Morton's nineteenth-place showing in the open race was not improved upon by an American until forty years later, long after competition shifted from open racing to time trials.

Morton was the California amateur champion for three years running, beginning in 1933 at age seventeen, while on his way to winning the 1936 U.S. Olympic Finals in Paterson, New Jersey.

"It rained so hard you couldn't see ten feet ahead," recalls Morton of the 100-kilometer (62.5 miles) race. A newspaper photograph of the five-foot-eight, 140-pounder churning ahead of the pack that day was recently reproduced as an oil painting by one of Morton's sons, and it has no trouble vying for space among the many bicycle knick-knacks decorating the Morton home.

Morton participated in football and baseball while at Polytechnic High School in his native Long Beach, but an introduction to the bicycle as a morning and evening newspaper delivery boy led him to concentrating on pedal pushing. "After that, I was never left out when it came to cycling," Morton said. "I made up my mind to do it, and I did. That's the secret in anything."

A three-hundred-mile-a-week training regimen was enough to gear him for the Olympics. But Morton knew that the elite European cyclists would be using three-speed bikes, something he had only heard about. He did manage to pack along a frame that he was told would adapt to the triple gears before departing for Olympic Village, just in case.

"Our team was pretty close going over," said Morton. "We had to be. All 410 of us were on board the SS *Manhattan* for six days. The trip totaled six weeks, two of which were on water. We didn't fly like they do now."

American swimmer Eleanor Holm, however, flew a little too high en route to Berlin. She was shelved from participation for drinking and partying. "We all felt bad about that," Morton said. "She was quite a competitor." The ship left New York Harbor on July 15, 1936, and when it docked, swimming champion Holm was kicked off the team. Most of the three hundred or so Olympians on board petitioned unsuccessfully for the world record holder in the one-hundred- and two-hundred-meter backstroke. "They said she got drunk. Well, so did a lot of others," said Morton. "It was a shame." Morton, nineteen years of age, competed in the Team Men's Road Race (won by France), Individual Men's Road Race (won by France's Robert Charpentier) and the four-thousand-meter Men's Team Pursuit (won by France).

Soon after the team arrived, Frenchman Oscar Egg, a cyclist who knew the Americans from races in the United States, approached Morton and said, "Here, Charley, you'll need this." Egg then passed out three-speed gears to the team.

"It was quite a shock," Morton recalls, "but I was fascinated. And I had a frame that it would fit. I had to laugh at some of the other guys. They had a heck of a time putting them on."

Morton later found that he preferred his customary one-speed over the three-speed combination. "It was too heavy," he said, "and it didn't give much variation, either."

Since neither the cycling team nor anyone else aboard ship had any real chance for workouts, with the exception of Miss Holm, it was time to hit the roads for some practice. The roads, however, were found wanting. "The German army strictly mapped out our practice roads," Morton recalled, "and they were awful. They were too narrow. Plus, it was cobblestone and granite. Some of the guys left the road and went through pigpens. I laughed when I heard the pigs start squealing. Boy, did we get it after that. A battalion of German soldiers picked us up, put us on a truck and took us back to the cobblestone. We learned what *verboten* meant."

The Olympic Village was located fifteen miles from Berlin. "It was really designed for Hitler's troops," Morton said. "It was put together very creatively, and I guess it served them quite well when we left." Female athletes, most of them swimmers, were housed forty miles opposite the men.

Capacity crowds filled the Olympiad each day. The atmosphere was festive. Overhead, the ill-fated, eight-hundred-foot-long zeppelin *Hindenburg* hovered while photographers recorded shots from its belly for world newspapers. The *Hindenburg* exploded less than a year later at the Naval Air Station at Lakehurst, New Jersey, killing all thirty-five aboard.

Morton toured Berlin's best restaurants and met its people after events ended for the day. The only barrier was the language. He even managed to get his picture in the Berlin daily newspaper while signing an autograph.

Dress uniforms for the American men consisted of straw hats and blue serge suits. White flannels were worn for parades. "I tried to save that straw hat, but I don't know what happened to it," Morton said. "I did save the suit, though."

Members of the '36 cycling team were Morton, Sinabaldi, Albert Schlesinger, Al Byrd, Paul Nixon, Coach Walter Grenda and alternate Buster Logan.

Morton was satisfied with his finish in the race. The French, as expected, finished first and second.

"I was glad to get what I did," Morton said. "We were bunched together at one point, and a bad spill cleared out most of the American team. I was so close to the front guys coming in. I had never competed against the Europeans, and it was a great thrill."

In 1937, Morton came back to win the U.S. amateur championship and placed second in the nationals in Atlantic City, New Jersey. With several relatives working in the Bakersfield oilfields, Morton moved to the area in 1939 and went to work as a bicycle mechanic at Vincent's Cyclery, at the same time turning pro with a debut at Madison Square Garden. His pro career was short-lived, however. The U.S. Army drafted him in 1940, and for the next five years, he served as an infantryman. It was while in the service that Morton met his wife of thirty-eight years, Katherine. He met her riding a bicycle.

"The pro racing circuit was more popular in the '30s than it is today," Morton says. "Back then, it was the big thing." Popular locations included the Pan Pacific and Civic Auditorium in Los Angeles and at Treasure Island near San Francisco.

Morton and other old-timers from the Long Beach Crebs Cycle Club still get together once a year for a reunion to celebrate bygone bicycle days.

A Canadian with flaming red hair, Torchy Peden was the best "six-day bike rider in the '30s." Something of an anomaly in a sport where the ideal

On the five-man U.S. Bicycle Team in the 1936 Olympics, Charles Morton still rides regularly with the Kern Wheelmen. *Author's collection.*

height is considered to be about six feet and a weight of more than 160 pounds is considered excess baggage, Peden stood six-foot-five and weighed over 200 pounds. "You definitely didn't want to run into him," Morton said. "He was the best six-day bike rider of his day. Now they call it 'six days of racing.' We used to run continuous around the clock. Now they start around two in the afternoon and knock off at midnight."

Afterword: In retirement, Morton stays active with the Kern Wheelmen. On his Vitus ten-speed, he rode fifty-two miles just to watch a ten-mile time trial sponsored by the Wheelman. He has also ridden to Ridgecrest, a 125-mile trip, and to Death Valley, a journey of nearly 220 miles. "I enjoy the scenery," he said.

Chapter 21

CHUCK ROBERSON AND A HORSE NAMED COCAINE: JOHN WAYNE'S DARING STUNT DUO

Bakersfield, April 13, 1975

Chuck Roberson, home from location in Bend, Oregon, paused to reflect on *Rooster Cogburn*, the *True Grit* sequel he finished recently with John Wayne. "You know, that's the first movie since 1950 that Cocaine and Wayne weren't together in," said Roberson.

Roberson was speaking about a horse named Cocaine, which he had ridden, à la John Wayne fashion, since he first began to "double" the famed actor back in 1948.

As he scattered some hay in a nearby stable situated on his spacious thoroughbred ranch headquartered in southeast Bakersfield, the conversation always returned to the memory of his late thirty-three-year-old friend. "I had to put him to sleep a few months ago," Roberson said, raising his six-foot-four frame to full height while studying a movement in the far depth of the paddock. "He was healthy otherwise, but he went blind, and I didn't want to see him hurt himself."

"Out there," Roberson pointed to a faraway pocket, "is Dollar." Dollar, he explained, was Cocaine's double, a "cast horse"—a quiet animal used for dialogue scenes. "Dollar is the horse Wayne rides," he said while opening a shed door and producing a large, brown leather saddle with "JOHN WAYNE" inscribed in gold letters.

"Duke?" He grinned. "Sure, sometimes I call him that. We're good friends. I probably get as much fan mail as he does; since we're together a lot, people get to know him and me as being a kind of team. And you know, he's still very athletic. Of course, at age sixty-seven, he has lost some of that great coordination he once had."

At that, Roberson, himself fifty-five, twists and turns his upper torso, relieving an old back injury, one of many in his long career as a "fall guy." In the meantime, his eighty-two-year-old father, Allie, exhibiting no such deterrents, pitches in on chores like a boomer looking for round-up duty.

"He sure is something," Roberson says in admiration of his agile dad. "I had him make the arrangements with Cocaine." When asked if he considered having the animal stuffed in the manner of Roy Rogers's Trigger, Roberson gave a visible grimace. "First, I wanted to have him buried right here, but then I realized the memory would be too much," he said. "I don't know what dad did with him, and I don't want to know."

The elder Roberson nodded, reiterating that he had also been concerned that the spirited animal might injure himself because of his sensory impairment.

So, with a part of the past now buried, Roberson back-stepped to the late '40s with a beginning much like the story of the boy who plucked the thorn from the lion's paw, thus prompting an immediate, lasting friendship between the two.

A young Roberson, born on a cattle ranch in Texas but now with stakes in the Los Angeles area, bought Cocaine after the previous owner discarded the seven-eighth thoroughbred due to a seemingly untreatable leg ailment. For seventy-four dollars, the remainder in delinquent veterinary fees, the horse was his. "His leg looked just awful," he recalled. "It was full of maggots and pus…just horrible looking and I couldn't bear to watch him limp."

At that, it wasn't exactly a gift horse. "It took about a year—a year and a lot of sunshine—and I cured him."

The former Flying H cowboy was predictably a horse fancier; the cure, however, also provided a remedy for a sore spot in his own life.

From a movie lot stable helper for Republic Studios, Roberson established himself as John Wayne's double in *The Fighting Kentuckians*. Then, in a later 1948 feature, *Rio Grande*, the stuntman lost a scene to another stuntman when he was unable to control his mount properly. He decided in that moment of chagrin to go horse hunting. A skilled apprentice, Cocaine gradually developed into one of the most sought-after "actors" in the business. Earnings in his lengthy equine life totaled more than $100,000.

There was no more stunting for the stuntman, doubling for the stand-in or backing up the double; Cocaine and Roberson were now a team, a duo subbing for John Wayne and Dollar (and many others) with their skilled acrobatics.

Hollywood stuntman Chuck Roberson and his trained horse, Cocaine, crash through a window in the movie *Chisum*. *Hancock House Publishers, 1980.*

John Wayne and his stunt double, Chuck Roberson, on a break in the shade while filming *The Shootist. Author's collection.*

"Cocaine was the best falling horse in the business," says Roberson. "He was also the best transfer horse. I would slow down to board a steam engine, and he never batted an eye."

"His demand got me a lot of parts," Roberson added. "I doubled Gregory Peck in *Big Country* and Clark Gable in *The Misfits* and broke both arms doubling for Vincent Price once. I guess I've doubled just about all of the big men: Randolph Scott, John Payne, Jeff Chandler and, for about twenty-five years, a fella named John Wayne."

Roberson makes it clear that he would not mistreat an animal for the sake of a thrilling movie scene. "Cocaine was well trained," he said. "He would fall or play dead at my cue. For years, we worked long hours to make the hard falls look realistic. There's still the chance that the sandpits are harder than you figured or that someone or something else will get in your way in the action scenes. There's still the danger. But well, Cocaine was a pro."

In addition to stuntman duty, Roberson has had several roles as an extra. He has also served as a second-unit director (action scenes) for *Beneath the Planet of the Apes* and as an action adviser in *How the West Was Won*, the picture that kept him employed for a year.

In *Taras Bulba*, Roberson made fifteen falls in one afternoon at $100 a fall. "Obviously, it's a profession you have to enjoy," he says. "The real danger—or my nemesis, anyway—has been in the makeshift fight scenes. You have to have proper equipment available to execute proper stunts and to minimize the element of injury."

Roberson admits to it having been a good career, and he talks now of spending more time at his ranch, where he stays between pictures, and looking after his Bay Meadows thoroughbred entry, Never Slippin'. He is a licensed thoroughbred trainer in both Washington and California.

He will get a call, sometime soon perhaps, for another Wayne episode. He still loves the work. It is the kind of work you have to love to keep getting up and dusting off the trousers. But he has eliminated a part of his skill. "No more falls," he says. "Just like an old thoroughbred, you can only run so long before you got to pull it up and rest awhile."

He will still double for Wayne, of course, and the other "big" men when his services are required. "But no more falls," he insists, rubbing his shoulder.

Movie Offers Little Action for Wayne's Stuntman

March 26, 1976

Director Don Siegel, at a Carson City, Nevada press gathering in early January, said his newest movie, a western titled *The Shootist*, would have a familiar plot but that the special star quality of John Wayne would raise it above the commonplace. "There will be very little action," he said.

As Bakersfield rancher-stuntman Chuck Roberson was to find out a couple weeks later when he arrived, Siegel was one director who followed his own lines to a "T."

Roberson came to do his thing just as he had in countless other action scenes, but even though the studio called him, it didn't use his talents in the little-action western. "I only put the clothes on once," Roberson said, referring to his Wayne look-alike togs, "and I could have postponed doing that."

Bakersfield rancher and stuntman Chuck Roberson paces on set in Carson City, Nevada, for the film *The Shootist. Photograph by author.*

Instead, Roberson basked in the unusually warm sun of mid-January as the clear, snow-tipped Sierra Nevada peaks provided a scenic backdrop from the window of his studio-financed room at the Ormsby House.

Being Wayne's exclusive stuntman since 1948 perhaps justified his being asked to do little else aside from simply showing up. "They always have a bunch of people they don't need," he points out. In *The Shootist*—a "fancy name for a gunslinger"—Wayne portrays a cancer-riddled sheriff who dies bravely. It will, no doubt, be one of those gentler passings since Roberson wasn't called for that scene, either.

Wayne's turn-of-the-century co-stars are Lauren Bacall and Ron Howard. Jimmy Stewart, Hugh O'Brien, Yaphet Kotto, John Carradine and Richard Boone round out the supporting roles. O'Brien did the role for free.

"Wayne called me recently," Roberson said. "In about three weeks, the picture will be finished. They're paying my horse $200 a week plus his feed. Heck, that's more than I'm making."

Cast and crew left the scenic Nevada city in late January and are now working in the backlot of the Warner Brothers studio, where Roberson's animal is earning his oats. Roberson, recently waylaid by a set of hitchhikers he befriended, is resting at his Bakersfield ranch from "a little concussion" and a painful injury that required

John Wayne emerges from the back entrance of the Ormsby House hotel after viewing Super Bowl X in his room on January 18, 1976. *Photograph by author.*

eight stitches in his eyeball. "Never again," he said, will he stop for a fellow human with his thumb up.

Roberson was thinking seriously about pitching his retirement bedroll in the Nevada town he just left. "I definitely was thinking about it until this came up," he said.

Roberson is already retired, but when Wayne beckons, he telephones the Screen Actors Guild and asks them not to send a check. The SAG will pay retirement benefits at fifty-five, so Chuck retired two years ago, with almost thirty years in the business.

"I did *Rooster Cogburn* last year, as well as some Disney work and Goldie Hawn's newest film, but I only work a little," said Roberson. Asked what the wages were for his kind of work, he said, "I started at about $200 a week; now the SAG requires a weekly minimum wage for a stuntman to be around $725. Actors make $80 less than that." He added, "Nobody, of course, works just for a minimum wage."

Although Roberson didn't receive any pseudo-blows from the bad men, he did draw three weeks' pay. "Even with my Wayne clothes on, I never got around to putting on the bowstring tie."

Which brings up the question: what's the difference between a double and a stuntman? "There really is no difference," Roberson said. "Both do action

Roberson admits that this is one movie with little demand for his stunt work, but when old pal John Wayne beckons, he responds. *Photograph by author.*

scenes and are never on camera long enough to be mistaken for anyone other than the person they are stunting for. The stand-in is different; he's just there to have the lights put on him."

Asked in Carson City why Wayne kept at it, Roberson said, "Because he likes to work—that's all."

Work is something that doesn't exactly go against Roberson's grain either, but he has other ways to earn greenbacks. "My horse, Never Slippin', finished second in the eighth race Thursday at Golden Gate," he said. "The day before, my filly, Ruler of the Sea, won by five lengths."

Afterword: Charles Hugh Roberson died on June 8, 1988, in a Bakersfield hospital, reportedly from cancer. He was sixty-nine years old. He left behind a wife, Dollie Mae, and four daughters. Prior to becoming Wayne's exclusive stuntman and a Hollywood legend, Roberson worked "ten-day Westerns" for Republic Studios in the 1940s. A daughter, Charlene, was a pioneer female makeup artist in the film industry.

Chapter 22

BIG NAMES FOR BUCK OWENS CELEBRITY GOLF

Bakersfield, 1974

Tom Kennedy, host of *Name That Tune*, won the fourth annual Buck Owens Pro-Celebrity Golf and Tennis Invitational tournament. Leading a star-studded celebrity field, John Wayne made a brief appearance, arriving in a helicopter. Charley Pride flew in from Salt Lake City just in time to close the entertainment show.

No other regular event held in Bakersfield has ever matched the star-power magnitude of Owens's annual charity tournament. It started out as just a golf tournament, but a Friday tennis tournament at the Bakersfield Racquet Club was added this year.

Fifty celebrities melded with a diverse bunch of current and former pro athletes from different sports.

Some of the celebrities over the years have been scratch golfers or better, such as Johnny Bench and Mickey Mantle.

The first Buck Owens Pro-Celebrity Invitational, held on November 1–2, 1971, included pro golfers Charlie Coody, the 1971 PGA Masters winner, and Bobby Nichols. Among the celebrities were Mantle, Joey Bishop, Maury Wills, Rusty Draper, Mickey Manners, Monty Hall, Glen Campbell, Charley Pride, Roy Rogers, Frank Cady, Willie Davis, Roy Rogers, George "Goober" Lindsey, Joey Bishop, Jim Davis and Congressman Bob Mathias, a former Olympic gold medalist in the decathlon.

A rendition of Owens's signature red, white and blue guitar was prominent on the program cover. The landmark Bakersfield Inn served as headquarters, while the tournament and banquet took place amid tall palms at the Bakersfield Country Club.

Crowd favorite mighty Mickey Mantle tees off as the gallery watches on a beautiful Saturday, November 2, 1974, during the annual Buck Owens charity golf tournament to raise money for cancer research. *Photograph by author.*

The format was "two best balls in foursome—full handicap." Additionally, only the golf professionals needed to keep an individual score. Divisions were pro, amateur and celebrity. The charity event netted $10,000 for cancer research that first year.

It was rare for fans and stargazers to see that many familiar faces roaming about so freely and accessible. The thirty-six-page program had two pages for autographs. While name recognition was a problem for some attendees, they overcame that handicap by asking anyone who looked like they might be a celebrity for their autograph.

In 1972, Bakersfield-born Dennis Ralston, captain and coach of the Davis Cup tennis team, won one of Owens's trademark guitars. The banquet show featured performers Mayf Nutter, Bob Morris, Stormy Winters, Buddy Alan, The Bakersfield Brass, Susan Raye, George Lindsey, Bobby John Henry and, of course, Owens and his Buckaroos band. A mix of entertainers and athletes included Bake Turner, Peter Marshall, Archie Campbell, Johnny Bench and Evel Knievel.

Another Olympic decathlon gold medal winner, Rafer Johnson, was all over the grounds at the Bakersfield Country Club in 1973. Johnson was vice-president of public affairs for Continental Telephone in Bakersfield.

Gallery tickets sold for one dollar each. Former New York Yankees baseball great Mickey Mantle was on hand again, along with Bobby Murcer, a Yankees centerfielder who came along after the "Commerce Comet." A longtime golfer, Mantle was known for his long drives. He was easy to spot with his blond hair and long-sleeved red cardigan.

Murcer placed second the previous year in the celebrity field. Buddy Hackett and Jackie Coogan could be seen trading quips. There was also Tennessee Ernie Ford and Foster Brooks. In all, 36 celebrity names topped the field out of 144 total entrants. A headline in the *Bakersfield Californian* read "6,000 Stargazers Take in Eyeful of Celeb Swingers."

Actor Telly Salavas and Joe Rudi from the Oakland A's won last year's tournament.

Dennis James and Norm Crosby looked enough alike to confuse some. Any time a celebrity got outside the restraining lines, they became engulfed in a sea of autograph seekers.

Mantle and Owens were old friends. In 1966, they were part of a pro-celebrity golf field competing in conjunction with the Country Music Festival held in Nashville and surrounding areas.

This year, Mayor Don Hart stood beside John Wayne and could have passed as his double. In addition to being similar in size, they were both college football linemen, Wayne at USC and Hart at Santa Barbara State.

Also present were Max Baer Jr., Robert Fuller, Efrem Zimbalist Jr., Arte Johnson, Ed Ames, John Amos, Lisa Todd, Ronnie Prophet, Larry Wilde and David Frizzell—again, the list of notables was long. Friday night was hospitality night at the Galley Room in the Bakersfield Inn.

Owens announced plans to build a cancer research center in Bakersfield. A grant in the amount of $176,000 was awarded for that development by the U.S. Department of Health, Education and Welfare in early September 1974.

Afterword: Owens held his tournament for four years, 1971–74. A two-year hiatus followed before Owens started the Buck Owens Rodeo Days in 1977. It ran for eight years and was a nine-day event when it ended. A dispute with the American Cancer Society branch in Bakersfield led to his cancelling the golf tournament after 1974. Heavily autographed programs from those tournaments, especially from the first one, in 1971, go for big bucks in Internet auctions.

Chapter 23

FORMER RODEO STAR NOW TOP ANIMAL TRAINER

Lebec, April 1976

Fess Reynolds trains various animals here at his ranch in Lebec. He has a dingo that has dropped a stick at my feet from its mouth and is looking up at me as if I should know what to do next. I'm watching Reynolds as he has Frosty, a full-grown Brahma bull, tethered and walking in a circle. The working area is a wide, shallow pit. The much-trampled ground is totally devoid of vegetation and rises slightly on an upslope all the way around.

You name the animal, and Reynolds has probably trained one here for movie work. Frosty is a minor movie star himself. I toss the stick with a strong throw, hoping the dingo might lose sight of it. Reynolds talks to me as he keeps Frosty moving slowly. I don't know what the regimen amounts to or how the training will be used. Some of his animals were utilized years ago by car dealer Cal Worthington for his late-night TV ads featuring his "dog" Spot, who was hardly ever a dog, but a tiger, camel or some other animal.

Reynolds is a common sight in the area, nestled in the pass region between the San Joaquin Valley and Los Angeles, running animals back and forth between Hollywood movie sets and his ranch. He became a traffic hazard of sorts because of all the gawkers. He said the California Highway Patrol (CHP) ordered him to quit hauling lions on his flatbed truck going down Highway 99 because of the distractions it caused to motorists and the potential for accidents. The dingo returns the stick back at my feet and continues its arrogant stare at me. I look at the stick, and it appears to be the same one. As I reach to pick it up, the dingo's head darts some toward my hand. I pick up the stick and really fling it this time.

Reynolds tells how his son "Jug" played the role of Little Beaver in the Red Ryder movies, replacing Robert Blake (known then as Bobby Blake). As Red Ryder's sidekick, Little Beaver was a lovable little Navajo boy whose catchphrase was "You betchum, Red Ryder," a phrase often uttered in my neighborhood and schoolyard in the early 1950s, when old cowboy reels filled our TV screens. Blake portrayed Little Beaver for all the Republic features from 1944 to 1947 with Bill Elliott as Red Ryder. Don Kay "Little Brown Jug" Reynolds followed as the last movie Little Beaver with Jim Bannon as Red Ryder.

"Roy Rogers brought me here with him," Reynolds said. He and his wife, Mable Lee, along with their young son Donald Kay, left Texas for California in the early 1940s. Rogers, known in the movies as "King of the Cowboys," sponsored a Wild West show in which Reynolds had participated.

In addition to being a top rodeo performer, Reynolds had bit parts in numerous Hollywood movies, nearly all of them westerns.

The author aboard a Brahma named Frosty at Fess Reynolds's ranch in Lebec. Reynolds trains various animals (mainly for movies) and is a former professional rodeo performer. *Photograph by Dave Bilyeu.*

Born in Texas around 1917, Reynolds was a consistent money winner in the rodeo circuit during the 1940s. His specialty was bull riding. He is short and stocky and looks like one of the many crusty sidekicks in those low-budget cowboy movies. He has another son, "Sled," who lives nearby and who also trains animals for movie work. All of his boys—I don't know how many—have been involved with the rodeo, stunt work and animal training most of their lives. The dingo drops the stick again. I bend to pick it up, and he clamps his teeth on my hand—not hard enough to break the skin, but a crushing pressure nonetheless. I pull my hand up as he releases his bite. I toss the stick for the last time.

"Go ahead, give Frosty a ride, why don't you?"

"How's your insurance?" I reply.

I climb on board, and the huge animal accepts me with nary a hint of reluctance. The dingo looks up at me with the stick in its mouth. I'm not falling for its tricks again.

Back on the ground again, Reynolds hands me a recent edition of the weekly trade publication *Circus Report*, which describes him as "one of the most unique and original acts in the world."

His act for hire includes a trained Brahma bull group of six (Bill, Charlie, Rico, Angel, Tommy and Jerry); Frosty, the "Comedy Bull," which starred in Walt Disney's *Twister, Bull From the Sky* in 1976 and in Sony Pictures' *For Pete's Sake* in 1974. Disney is a regular Reynolds client. He trained a bear for the studio at his Lebec ranch in the late 1950s for a part in *Old Yeller*.

A "Six Pony Liberty Act" and a "Six Brahman Liberty Act" is sometimes part of his show. The word "liberty" in circus context means the animals respond to verbal commands and are not restrained by reins. They are "at liberty."

The CHP might have cut him some slack in not ticketing him with a public-nuisance citation due to the fact that Reynolds often appeared at the annual Kern County Rodeo in Bakersfield, going back as far as 1945, when his show featured "his two star riding children." The rodeo was sponsored by the Kern County unit of the CHP.

Walking to my car to leave, it dawns on me. The dingo, possibly having picked up some tips from his master, trained me well.

Afterword: Reynolds died in 2000 at age eighty-four. His sons have carried on the animal training tradition.

Chapter 24
Mayor Turns Cowboy Life into Song

Bakersfield, August 8, 1975

Bakersfield mayor Donald M. Hart welcomed me into his downtown office. He introduced his "high school football coach," Buddy Cummings, who was visiting. He remained during the interview.

Immediately, the phone rang, and the mayor spoke in a slightly exaggerated Irish tongue to an apparent close friend. "I've been deer hunting," he said. "Now I shoot 'em up the hill so they roll down. Damn if I'm gonna pack 'em around on my back anymore," he laughed.

Hart is thick chested, broad shouldered and has a modest midriff bulge. He was a college boxer and a football center at Santa Barbara State Teachers College under Coach Theodore "Spud" Harder and was a member of that school's 1936 conference-championship team that went 9–1. Coach Harder earned his nickname while selling potatoes as a kid in his hometown of Bakersfield. Hart played football at Bakersfield Junior College for Harder and made the move with him to Santa Barbara.

Hart soon ended the call and hung up the phone. "Well, we're not getting very far with the interview, are we?" He was as cordial making the apology as he was in OK'ing the interview after I called him a couple days ago. I had heard through the grapevine he had written a song that Buck Owens had published. I asked him about the song. "Oh, that," he said, amused. "Buddy here knows all about those 'thirty and found' days, and so do I. You see, I called Bob Morris at the Buck Owens place and told him I had some lyrics. He asked me to read them. So I read them over the phone, and he liked them. He later put music to it, and I haven't heard anything since."

A gifted athlete in several sports, Don Hart was an all-around sportsman, as evidenced by this large marlin he brought in while fishing with brother-in-law Jim Camp (far right) and Saul A. Camp employee George Sakai. *Author's collection.*

Hart was a U.S. Army Air Force officer in World War II and a part of the China-Burma-India Theater with an Air Transport Command (ATC) base unit in India. Morris, the manager for Owens's music publishing house in Oildale, may have liked the lyrics, but he was not certain what some of them alluded to. "The 'thirty and found' threw him," Hart said, as he cast a knowing glance at Cummings. "See, that was a cowboy's wages, thirty dollars a month and whatever he could find. Buddy knows—he worked for a dollar a day and got two dollars and fifty cents for every horse he broke… that last part was found money. I worked forty and found. I guess most people wouldn't know about things like that."

In 1962, *Sports Illustrated* named Hart to its Silver Anniversary All-America football team, recognizing former athletes who went on to distinguish themselves in other fields, including public service.

Hart married Margaret Willene Camp, daughter of wealthy California rancher Saul A. Camp, who built a harness-racing empire in Kern County. Camp was the leading harness-racing horse owner in America in 1956, due largely to the feats of his prize trotter, Scott Frost, and the skill of harness racer Joe O'Brien.

Hart summoned his secretary and asked her to get me a copy of his song. I questioned if he was trying to capitalize on the current popularity of country music and Owens's clout and popularity within the commercial country music industry. "You can take that approach about me if you like," he said, "but I didn't get caught up in anything. I've been writing poems for years. It's a delicate way to express yourself in times of stress. I have drawers full of them. Don't forget, I'm Irish, and being a poet is part of being Irish."

His secretary came forth and handed me a copy of the lyrics to "I'm a Rodeo Hand."

"Have you got music for it?" I asked.

"They're taking care of that," he said.

I thanked the mayor, and as I drove home, I turned the radio to KUZZ, the Owens-owned station. I wondered if I would someday hear the mayor's cowboy song. I would have to wait—just like him.

Afterword: Hart died on July 11, 2002, at eighty-seven years of age. He retired in 1980 as mayor after serving three terms. Don Hart Drive, on the campus of Cal State Bakersfield University, is named for him.

Chapter 25

Rosi Reed Captures Women's World Boxing Title

Bakersfield, June 1980

With the Women's Boxing Board (WBB) crowning a new flyweight champion on May 30 at Strongbow Stadium in Bakersfield's Rosi Reed, a question arises: who is the WBB?

Reed won the title, which was vacant, from number-one ranked Bonnie Prestwood of Indiana. Prestwood, however, is still the Women's Boxing Federation (WBF) champion and also holds the title with the World Women's Boxing Association (WWBA).

The organization with the most prestige appears to be the WBB, according to its organizers. "We're about the only credible sanctioning body at present," Johnny Dubliss, WBB president, said from his ringside seat at Strongbow. "The others aren't that active."

With Dubliss was chairwoman Beverly Patrick, excited about the size of the crowd, estimated at one thousand, and the prospect of handing out an impressive title belt.

"Isn't it great?" she beamed, scanning the tiers of full seats in the ancient dome-roofed stadium.

The most well known of all female boxers is Cat Davis, but Dubliss says the tall beauty is no drawing card. "Cat has drawn about two hundred for each of her last two fights," he said. "She's had all the media hype, but she can't pack them in."

Prestwood, by the way, a game but sorely inadequate boxer, as she showed at Strongbow, owns a win over Ernestine Jones, who defeated Davis in an upset.

At 108 pounds, Rosi Reed was relentless in pummeling Indiana-based Bonnie Prestwood on the way to a sixth-round TKO and a $1,000 purse. *Photograph courtesy Tony Reed.*

Promoter Beverly Patrick fits the gold championship belt on Rosi Reed after the Bakersfield flyweight captured the Women's Boxing Board world championship title at Strongbow Stadium. Referee Marty Denkin makes it official. *Photograph courtesy Tony Reed.*

Dubliss, a Los Angeles–area resident, said the WBB formed as an offshoot of the WWBA. The WWBA began by staging popular all-women cards at the Hyatt Lake Tahoe Hotel about two years ago. Dubliss and a partner, Joe Bradley, felt it was time to take the show on the road, but when other directors nixed that idea, the WBB was born.

The decision didn't hurt his feelings any. "Some of the managers at Lake Tahoe would hide silver dollars on their girls so they could make weight," he said. "I know the ones who did it, and it wasn't my style. I like an honest organization. Pulitzer said the three most important things in journalism are accuracy, accuracy and accuracy, and that's my philosophy with the WBB."

With that said, he announced that the WBB rankings are scheduled for publication in coming issues of *Boxing Illustrated* and *Ring* magazines. "We had to pay to get them in *Ring*," he conceded. "Prestwood's record is 10–4, not 11–2. Promoters like to change things around, but that is her true record."

According to Patrick, the flyweight title bout was originally to be between Prestwood and the number-two contender. But Reed, ranked third, got the nod when the number-two contender "backed out."

"It's not unusual that Reed, with just two fights, is ranked so high," Patrick said. "It's hard to find women in that weight class. Experience counts, but so does ability, and we feel that Rosi has the ability."

Reed's impressive sixth-round TKO settled any doubts.

Prestwood and Reed had a common opponent in Karen Bennett. For Reed, it was a mismatch. Reed was a true flyweight and maybe even a weight classification lower. Bennett was a bantamweight and outweighed Reed by at least fifteen pounds, plus she was a more seasoned boxer. Why, then, did the fight take place in the first place?

"I was green…I was dumb," said Rosi's husband, Tony. "I didn't think weight mattered that much."

Rosi fought under the name "Rosetta Cappello."

"We wanted a name that sounded mafia bad…scary," said Tony.

The bout was held at the Silver Slipper in Las Vegas in 1977. Bennett was declared a knockout winner in the first round when Rosi (then fighting as Rosetta) quit.

"Rosi was landing punches, but she did not like the situation," Tony said.

Prestwood lost to Bennett on November 24, 1978. At one time, Bennett was the number-one bantamweight contender.

Reed and Prestwood probably looked like they had rubber legs during the bout.

"The maintenance man installed wrestling pads instead of boxing pads," said Tony. "It was like a trampoline. That could wear out the legs of someone like Rosi, who moved around a lot. After the fight, I brought it to the attention of Harry Kabakoff, and he was really upset that such a thing happened."

The fight had been postponed from an original date for three to four months due to an illness suffered by Rosi.

Rosi had fought at Strongbow previously, on October 23, 1978, when she defeated Nancy Thompson. The main event was a double matchup: Ruben Castillo v. Juan Batista and Gonzalo Montellano v. "King Cobra" Carbin. Castillo entered the ring at 31–0, and Montellano was 17–0. Castillo was managed by Raul Garza, a former promoter for Mexican dances in Bakersfield. Garza took over from Harold Cox Sr., a Bakersfield liquor store owner. Castillo's record was 20–0 when he left Cox.

Kabakoff (real name Melville Himmelfarb), a boxing trainer, manager and promoter, was known as the premier handler of Mexican fighters in the United States. He died in 2009 at age eighty-two in a Northridge, California hospital. In his *Los Angeles Times* obituary, he was remembered by boxing publicist Bill Caplan as "maybe the most colorful character in boxing that I've ever met, and everyone in boxing is colorful."

Afterword: Today, Rosi Reed is a Bakersfield attorney. Prestwood died at age fifty-three in her native Indiana. She reportedly suffered from pugilistic dementia. Denkin is the only referee to ever count out Rocky Balboa (Sylvester Stallone) in the movies. In *Rocky III*, a battered and groggy Balboa goes down for the count, called out by Denkin. It was the only time Rocky was knocked out in the popular movie series. The blow came from Clubber Lang (Mr. T). Prestwood, from Muncie, Indiana, was nicknamed the "Iron Maiden." Reed and her husband, Tony, owned the newspaper the *Rosedale Roadrunner*. She wrote a column for the newspaper titled "A Ring for Rosi." Each column showed a picture of her holding a phone to her ear. Kabakoff begin promoting fights in Bakersfield in earnest beginning in 1977.

BAKERSFIELD HAS RICH BOXING HISTORY

Bakersfield is a city with a boxing history. Light heavyweight Frank Daniels was an Olympic alternate in 1948. In a rare boxing match staged at Sam

Lynn Ballpark on August 2, 1955, Daniels, a former marine, defeated Frankie Haynes. Daniels's manager was Archie Moore.

Bakersfield country music singer Ronnie Sessions's older brother, Rick, was a boxer. There was also the mythical Aurelio Herrera, "Bad Billy" Wagoner and Tony "Toro" Noriega.

Bakersfield liquor store owner Harold Cox Sr. had a stable of boxers, but one stood out from the rest: Ruben Castillo.

Castillo failed to cash in on any of his four title matches. Still, he was regarded as one of the best in his day, and after retiring from the ring, he made a name for himself as a television fight commentator.

Denkin and Castillo go back some. In addition to working some of Castillo's adult fights as a referee and a judge, Denkin was the youth center director at China Lake starting in 1969. In that capacity, he often promoted junior and senior boxing matches on the navy base, one of which, on December 6, 1969, pitted an eleven-year-old, sixty-five-pound Castillo against a more seasoned Frank Baltazar Jr. Actor Audie Murphy presented some of the boxing awards that evening.

THE FIGHTING QUARRY BROTHERS

Heavyweight champion contender Jerry Quarry was born in Bakersfield on May 15, 1947, and his two brothers, Mike and Robert, were also well known for their pro boxing exploits. Mike ran a restaurant at one time in Bakersfield, where Robert was often in trouble with the law. While Johnny Callison is considered the best baseball player to ever come out of Bakersfield, Jerry Quarry is thought by many to be the best heavyweight to have never held the title. His nicknames were "Irish" and the "Bellflower Bomber," the latter coming by virtue of his growing up there. *Ring* magazine hailed Quarry as the most popular boxer during the peak of his career, 1969–71. With his blond hair and good looks, he appeared in small television and movie roles during his heyday. His father put the gloves on him at an early age. He won the 1965 Golden Gloves championship held in Kansas City, Missouri, at age nineteen. In a feat still unmatched, he knocked out all five of his opponents. His overall record was 53–9–4. Two of those losses came against Muhammad Ali, while another two were to Joe Frazier. His best shot at the title was when he lost to Jimmy Ellis. Other losses came against Ken Norton and George Chuvalo. Quarry had notable wins over Earnie Shavers, Ken

Muhammad Ali came out of a three-year exile on October 26, 1970, to take on the "Great White Hope," Bakersfield-born heavyweight Jerry Quarry, in a bout won by Ali in Atlanta. Author's collection.

Lyle, Mac Foster, Buster Mathis, Thad Spencer and Floyd Patterson. One of his draws also came against Patterson. His only fight in Bakersfield was held on November 22, 1983, when he defeated James Williams at the fairgrounds. Quarry died on January 3, 1999, and is buried in the Shafter Cemetery in Shafter, just outside Bakersfield.

Jerry Quarry also had a nickname—one he did not care for—given to him by the press: "The Great White Hope." The nickname was a reference to the dominance of black fighters in that era, especially in the heavyweight division. The phrase "The Great White Hope" started in the early 1900s with the emergence of black heavyweight Jack Johnson. Large sums of money were offered to white fighters to take on Johnson. Ironic is the fact that Johnson was living in Bakersfield in 1902, when he fought the first meaningful fight of his career against Jack Jeffries, brother of heavyweight champ Jim Jeffries. Jim publicly stated he would not fight Johnson. Johnson had knocked out Jack and, according to old news accounts, turned to Jim, who was at ringside, and said, "I can whip you, too." Jim retired without the two ever pairing. Six years after he retired, however, Jim came out of retirement and agreed to battle Johnson, who was now the heavyweight champion. The fight took place in Reno, Nevada, in 1910, and Johnson won by TKO in what was billed as the "Fight of the Century."

Light heavyweight Mike Quarry, also born in Bakersfield, died on June 11, 2006, at age fifty-three. He was 24–2–2 as an amateur and 62–13–6 as a pro from 1969 to 1982. In 1972, he lost to Bob Foster in a title match. It was a co-feature with his brother Jerry going against Ali.

Bobby Quarry, the sole surviving Quarry boxer brother and the only one not a Bakersfieldian by birth (he was born in Lynwood, California), was 9–12–2 with six knockouts fighting as a heavyweight from 1982 to 1992. Bobby, forty-three, was released in November 2006 from Folsom State Prison, where he was serving a sentence for grand theft. Jimmy Quarry, the eldest brother, had one pro fight. He was knocked out and never fought again.

Chapter 26
MOON AND THE LEGENDARY LEATHERHEADS

Taft, March 31, 1978

Vern "Moon" Mullen will be among those invited to the annual weeklong NFL Alumni meeting beginning this weekend in Fort Lauderdale, Florida.

Mullen played five years in the old NFL beginning with the Canton Bulldogs in the team's 1923 championship year and later with the Chicago Bears, Chicago Cardinals and Pottsville Maroons.

George "Papa Bear" Halas, Art Rooney and Pete Rozelle are the first to receive the symbolic gold lapel pin in the shape of a leather football helmet with a solitaire diamond set in the side. The pin represents the long-obsolete headgear worn by players in football's formative years. The NFL Alumni formed in 1967 to deal with player welfare issues.

The legendary Halas and Mullen each played the end position, sometimes on both offense and defense. Halas was owner, head coach and player for the Bears. "Halas was a terrific guy," said Mullen. "He was tougher than a boot on the field, and on the sidelines, he ripped and roared up and down the bench."

Mullen, seventy-eight, hopes to see many of his old teammates in Florida. He was born in Illinois, where he played football at Taylorville High and, later, for the University of Illinois. "My coach at Taylorville said next to my brother Dean, I was the best player he ever had," Mullen recalled.

Mullen then told how, in a sixty-minute game for Taylorville, Dean scored twenty-two touchdowns in a 181–0 whipping.

At Illinois, Mullen said he remembers playing against Duke Slater, the first black All-America football player at Iowa.

Highly heralded Red Grange (fur coat) with Vern "Moon" Mullen to his left on the Chicago Bears bench during a game against Packers on November 22, 1925. Grange was slated to debut with the Bears in a game on Thanksgiving Day. *Author's collection.*

The biggest headlines in those days, however, were reserved for another Illini player turned professional: Red "The Galloping Ghost" Grange.

In 1925, Grange sat on the bench alongside Mullen wearing a pre–Joe Namath raccoon coat. It was only a day after Grange's great and final college game against Ohio State. Now a Bear, Grange would suit up next Thursday in his pro debut at Cubs Field.

Grange attracted the Bears' first sellout crowd in his debut. In 1925–26, he went on to star in an unbelievable barnstorming tour that produced large crowds and millions of dollars in revenue.

"In 1926, eighty-three thousand people filled the Coliseum in Los Angeles," Mullen recalled. "Grange got 40 percent of the gate. He cleaned up when it came to money. And Saturday, they closed down all the stores and had a parade for us."

Mullen does not like to mention his salary. He does admit to his first year in the league as being the one in which he was paid the most. "That was because the owners were richer that year," he said.

The NFL Alumni is helping to right the needs of pioneer players. "If you played just a year in the league, and if you're needy, they'll help you," said Mullen, who gets no retirement money from his playing days. "We were supposed to get a pension three years ago. The players struck and revised the plan and left out everyone who played before 1958. They usurped our funds, but we have a lawsuit. The only thing good is that they did lower the retirement benefit age to fifty-five. A straight pension would be better. I think it'll come. Look at the revenue they're getting from television. Then there's what they call the 'dire-need fund' that comes from the owners' pockets. After you're evaluated as being needy, they supplement your income up to $10,000 per year."

Mullen's last year in the old NFL was in 1927. He then joined a four-team winter league that played in the coastal areas, teams such as George Wilson's Wildcats and Red Grange's Yankees. Jim Thorpe was on one of the teams.

First National Studios in Hollywood shot footage from one of Grange's games and made it into a movie, one of several Grange and team members participated in as fringe benefits. One of the films, Mullen said, was "a parody done on *Ben-Hur* [silent film, 1925]."

Mullen kept his football gear stored in the same locker rooms as baseball's Chicago Cubs. "We played on the Chicago Cubs' baseball field and used their clubhouse," he said. "It was really something to get to look around and see all the familiar names on the lockers. Some really stood out."

Some of those names would have included Gabby Hartnett, Rabbit Maranville, Sheriff Blake and Grover Alexander.

"We practiced and then left when the baseball players came in," he said. "You know," Mullen looked up as if he had just remembered it, "I never did stay over to see a baseball game."

In 1929, Mullen took a position as head of the physical education department at Taft Union High School, a post he held for thirty-four years. He was athletic director at the high school and at Taft Junior College simultaneously for twenty-three of those years.

Mullen scored one touchdown during his pro career, in a 10–7 win at Navin Field in Detroit on October 3, 1926. Quarterback Paddy Driscoll got the Bears out in front in the opening period with a pass to Mullen at midfield. The Bear end raced fifty yards into the end zone for a touchdown, and Driscoll added the extra point.

When Grange was doing poorly, perhaps in a twist to change his luck, he swapped his coonskin coat and fancy fedora for Mullen's distressed felt hat and plain overcoat. His play picked up, and he again began to live up to his billing.

Vern Elmo Mullen was born in Taylorville, Illinois, on February 27, 1900. In addition to Illinois, he also attended West Virginia Wesleyan College, excelling in football. At six feet and 185 pounds, he played end and halfback.

In 1930, when Taft was the San Joaquin Valley champion, the rivalry between Valley neighbors Taft and Bakersfield was keen. Emotions tied with the rivalry led to a 1980 movie titled *The Best of Times*, starring Kurt Russell. Key scenes were filmed in Taft.

Mullen married a 1930 Taft High School grad, Lorraine Passehl. Lorraine played the trombone in the high school's all-girl band that marched in the Pasadena Tournament of Roses Parade in 1928, 1929 and 1930.

Mullen may have been the "original Moon," as he stated in our interview, or he may have meant that he was the first well-known person nicknamed after the popular comic-strip character Moon Mullins, a series that launched in 1923.

Afterword: Moon Mullen died at age eighty on September 14, 1980, in Taft.

Chapter 27
THE BEST OF TIMES

Taft, 1986

In January 1985, crew members for the pseudo-documentary movie *The Best of Times* began arriving in numbers in Taft. The writer of the film, Ron Shelton, is the son of Rathburn "Rath" Wiley Shelton, a 1941 graduate of Taft Union High School, and the former Peggy Emmens. The Shelton family lived at the Honolulu Oil Co. lease northeast of Taft on the north side of 36-Hill.

A young Shelton learned about the rivalry between Taft and Bakersfield from his father and grandparents. Rath, a top athlete in his day, later moved to Santa Barbara.

Taft, about thirty miles west-southwest of Bakersfield, was founded in 1888. In 1888, it was known as Moron. The name was changed to Taft in 1912. Town historian Pete Gianopulos was born in 1924, making him only slightly younger than the town bearing the Taft name. (Gianopulos, a 1942 Taft Union graduate and classmate of Rath Shelton, started a newsletter in 1994. He generously allowed me to use some of his recollections in this book.) He offers the following memories of the filming of the movie:

> *When Rath came to Taft in the fall of 1984, he would always stop by to see me. I was the Director of Guidance at Taft High at the time. He always had questions about who to contact around Taft for the various locations that would be needed. Rath always referred to me as "Deep Throat" for helping him with the information that was needed before the filming could begin.*

The filming took about two weeks, although parts of the movie were filmed elsewhere.

During the filming here in Taft, many people from the area would watch the filming, and some even had bit parts in the movie. One thing that was very nice was how close the spectators could get to the filming area and see the stars doing their thing.

Another thing that I remember was that Goldie Hawn spent some time here, and she and Kurt Russell could be seen together in one of the local restaurants eating in a secluded corner.

Relying on a fantasy theme of going back in time to make amends for a past misdeed, Jack Dundee (Robin Williams) is a milquetoast banker living in Taft, unable to erase the memory of a 1972 high school football game between Taft and powerhouse Bakersfield. Dundee muffed a perfect pass from quarterback and friend Reno Hightower (Kurt Russell), and the game ended in a tie. Dundee wants to bring his fantasy to life and replay the game. It takes some convincing to persuade Hightower and the townsfolk, so he resorts to desperate measures to make the game a reality.

Reno Hightower: "Half these people came here tonight, Jack, to watch you catch the ball. The other half came to see you drop it. You drop that damn thing again, Jack, your life is over."

Excitement brewed as the time neared for the movie's release. You could even say some of the thrill is cemented in history, as Gianopulos relates:

Some months later, when the editing was completed, the producers, the director, Roger Spottiswoode, Ron and Rath Shelton had a movie premier, and The Best of Times *was shown in Taft's Fox Theater—a gala event in Taft. Being there, what stands out in my mind while watching this motion picture was the laughter (it is a comedy) but also when the audience recognized the locations and the filming of the various scenes and the local people who were in the movie.*

The evidence that Robin Williams and Kurt Russell were here is cast in cement. It just happened that they were laying some cement between the curb and the sidewalk on the southeast corner of 6th and North Streets in the downtown area of Taft. To the south of North Street at this location was vacant lot where trailers had been parked. This is where the actors would go when they were not required to be on camera.

As they walked by that corner and saw the wet cement, Robin Williams, Kurt Russell and others in the crew took advantage of this opportunity to

COLORFUL ATHLETES OF THE CENTRAL VALLEY

do some writing and place their handprints, foot prints, etc., to immortalize the occasion for history. Robin Williams wrote his name and also wrote, "You're in good hands with Jack Dundee"—the name of the character that he played in the movie. He also planted his two hands in the wet cement. The bottoms of Kurt Russell's shoes appear in the cement in addition to his name.

And there in the cement is the proof of that occasion in early 1985 when Hollywood came to Taft.

Although the bulk of the movie was filmed in areas of Taft Union High School at several Center Street locations, as well as the 200 block of Sixth Street, 615 Shattuck Avenue and elsewhere, the big game was shot at Moorpark Memorial High School in Moorpark, California. The names of the teams that faced off in the match were the Bakersfield Tigers and the Taft High Rockets. In actuality, Taft Union High is the Wildcats, and Bakersfield High is the Drillers. Actress Robyn Lively made her debut in the film. Roger Spottiswoode, the director and a Canadian, was not altogether familiar with American football. His wife, Holly Palance, daughter of actor Jack Palance and Virginia Baker, played the role of Elly Dundee (spouse of Jack Dundee). It was the first sports film written by Ron Shelton. His next film project was as director of *Bull Durham*. Jack Palance, interestingly, was a Tehachapi resident from 1964 until his death in 2006 and a former heavyweight pro boxer under the name Jack Brazzo.

A Disney film star as a youngster, Kurt Russell played second base in the early 1970s for California Angels minor-league affiliates the Bend Rainbows, the Walla Walla Islanders, the Portland Mavericks and the El Paso Sun Kings. While with AA El Paso in the Texas League in 1973, Russell sustained a rotator-cuff injury to his throwing arm, sidelining his diamond days and prompting a return to acting. He did make a final cameo baseball appearance in 1977 in one game for the Portland Mavericks, an independent in the Northern League. On that same Portland team was Terry Lee, who would later have productive plate years in 1978 and 1979 with the Bakersfield Outlaws.

Shelton played minor-league baseball from 1967 to 1971. In 1969, he was a teammate of Arvin's Junior Kennedy while with the Stockton Ports of the California League. Kennedy went on to have a Major League career encompassing seven years, primarily with the Cincinnati Reds.

TAFT VERSUS BAKERSFIELD WAS ONCE KEEN HIGH SCHOOL RIVALRY

The high school rivalry between Taft and Bakersfield was natural due to the proximity of the two communities and the fact that they were one-time conference foes. Some of that town rivalry existed as a carryover when it came to junior college football, but to a far lesser extent. Both schools excelled at the junior-college level.

Bakersfield High has won more state football titles than any other school in California.

The Potato Shrine Bowl (or "Spud Bowl") is usually associated as being played at Memorial Stadium in Bakersfield. It was held there starting with the first one in 1948 and for most years thereafter. However, the 1949 Potato Bowl was battled out in Taft with Boise Junior College (Idaho) defeating home-team Taft. Bakersfield won the 1957 Potato Bowl.

Junior Rose Bowl games were held in Pasadena starting in 1946. That run ended in 1966 and gave way to the Pasadena Bowl. In the 1967 Pasadena Bowl, San Fernando Valley State was paired with West Texas State and Mercury Morris. Poor attendance brought the end of the Pasadena Bowl in 1971. In 1976, the Junior Rose Bowl resurfaced. Bakersfield Junior College won Junior Rose Bowl games held in Pasadena in 1953, 1959 and 1976.

Competition for state junior college titles has Taft with four (1938, 1982, 1984, 1990) and Bakersfield with six (1953, 1959, 1961, 1976, 1988, 2012). Taft College, of course, ceased its football program in 1994. Taft won national football championships in 1937 and in 1977 as ranked by Harry C. Frye (HCF). Taft won two more national titles based on the JC Grid-Wire in 1982 and 1984.

Al Baldock was the Taft College head coach from 1976 to 1993, compiling a 137–26–5 record with JC Grid-Wire national championships in 1982 and 1984. Under his guidance, Taft won Division II state championships in 1977 and 1979. Baldock was an All-American end at USC. His roommate was Bakersfield-raised Frank Gifford.

Chapter 28

THE BASEBALL SAGA OF BUCKSHOT MAY

Bakersfield, 1981

William "Buckshot" May admits to being a green kid when a big-time baseball scout approached him, but he did not hesitate in speaking his mind when he felt a legendary baseball team owner reneged on a promise.

While Joe Fan does not seem to favor the Major League Baseball Players' Association threatened May 22 walkout if players and owners fail to reach a contract compromise by that date, one old-timer backs those in uniform all the way. "Baseball owners are finally getting a dose of the same medicine they've dished out all these years," says eighty-year-old May, the first baseball player born in Bakersfield to turn professional at a major level.

May has little sympathy for the magnates of baseball. While not totally agreeing with all the players' demands, he vividly recalls when players were relegated to near-slavery status. That changed when the reserve clause, binding a player to one team for perpetuity, was lifted a few years back.

"They [the owners] would say, 'Do it or find some pick-and-shovel work.' There were no in-betweens," said May, who still lives in Bakersfield.

A gangly right-hander with a wicked screwball, May hurled for the Pittsburgh Pirates in 1924. He was a sensation in the Pirates' spring training camp held at Paso Robles after winning eighteen games at Omaha in his second pro season. If he made the big club, owner Barney Dreyfuss had promised a raise over his $400 a month salary.

"That was peanuts," May scoffed, wincing at the recall. "You could make that much in A ball. I asked for $800 after I made the club. I would have taken anything above that, but they wouldn't talk to me anymore about a raise."

He made the big club, but the raise never came. He complained and was sent packing. May went back to the minors and racked up some big winning seasons, but the call never came to rejoin the big time. Was he blacklisted by Dreyfuss?

"I don't know," he replied. "But I do know that when an owner had it in for you in those days, he really fixed you. And when you were gone, you weren't heard from again. I kinda gave up after having good years and not getting called up."

But he did get his raise. The Opening Day pitcher for the San Francisco Seals of the Pacific Coast League a year later, May's contract called for $600 a month. In 1926, he held out for $850 until the initial game and got it.

For the Pirates, May's historical contribution was minimal: one inning, one strikeout, no walks, two hits allowed, no runs and no decision. Nevertheless, he was with Pittsburgh until July 4, nearly two and a half months.

The '24 Pirates were a free-spirited, rollicking bunch who made almost as many headlines off the field as on. May fit right in.

"I finally had a showdown with Dreyfuss," May said. "He told me I hadn't pitched enough. I got mad and mimicked his Jewish accent, saying, 'Vel, ve don't keep our promises, do ve?' I was sent to Oklahoma City."

From 1922 to 1935, May compiled a 178–136 won-loss record in the minors. Few pitchers today throw a screwball, a curveball that breaks the other way, mainly because it is hard to control and damaging to a pitcher's arm. The great Carl Hubbell was the foremost practitioner of the pitch during May's era. May and Hubbell were teammates at Oklahoma City in 1924 and 1925.

A 1924 spring report from the *Pittsburgh Post* newspaper stated, in part, "Unsung and unheralded, Buckshot has jumped into prominence over his exploited pals by his unexpected skill, sheer courage and devil-may-care bearing off the field. On the field, Buckshot is all business."

From another report: "Every time a rookie pops up with the Pittsburgh club who draws the focus by characteristics other than diamond traits, the 1924 medal goes to Buckshot May, the tall boy from Bakersfield, Calif. Buckshot is a picturesque native whose effervescence reflects the California sunshine."

Five of May's teammates—Max Carey, Kiki Cuyler, Rabbit Maranville, Burleigh Grimes and the great Pie Traynor—are in baseball's Hall of Fame in Cooperstown, New York. Another on that list is manager Bill "Deacon" McKechnie, who lived up to his nickname when he once shuttled the whole team to hear a sermon by famous evangelist Billy Sunday.

There is a tinge of regret after all these years regarding May's confrontation with Dreyfuss. "I would have been in the '25 World Series if I had kept my mouth shut," he said. Pittsburgh defeated Washington in that contest.

May earned his nickname from wildness early in his career, first as "Scattershot," which was later changed by his peers to "Buckshot."

In hitting his stride as a pitcher, May mastered a change-up, developed control and added a screwball, a pitch taught to him by Babe Adams. May later showed Carl Hubbell how to throw the "screwgie."

After topping all pitchers in the Western League for St. Joseph, Missouri, in 1933, with a 24–6 record, May sat out the 1934 season to work in the Taft oilfields, a job he had held in off-seasons throughout his baseball years. He was offered a managing job at Cedar Rapids in the 1936 season, but an oilfield accident that left one of his feet partially dismembered cost him that Class A position.

As an oilfield superintendent, May traveled the world after leaving baseball; remaining a diamond fan and reading box scores wherever he could find a newspaper. The game, he says, has changed for the worse in some respects. "They're making too much money today, and they won't take chances like they used to," he said. "Catchers don't block the plate as they should. They make so much money they don't want to get hurt. It's bad for baseball. Also, players get more daily meal money than most people make in wages. We got three dollars a day. It was a big problem with the owners when I played. If you gave it to a player in cash, he was apt to get tight with it and starve himself. If they set up a meal table, players would eat too much and get out of shape."

May has many stories about baseball and the men who played it; some of the best are about him. "I was a raw kid playing the sandlots in Bakersfield," he said. "This Seattle scout came up to me—and this shows you how green I was—'Are you free?' he asked. 'No, I'm married,' I told him. He said he didn't mean that. He wanted to know whom I was connected with. I told him I worked for Associated Oil. It's a wonder he ever signed me."

Afterword: The strike May referred to in 1981 began on June 12 and forced the cancellation of 38 percent of the Major League schedule before play resumed on August 9. An early trading card of May with Seattle is a part of the 1922 Zee-Nut series. Another card in that series is of the legendary Jim Thorpe, then with the nearby Portland Beavers team. The Seattle Indians of the Pacific Coast League often held baseball tryouts in Kern County. The Pittsburgh Pirates held their first spring camp in Paso Robles in 1924. In 1926, they established a winter camp in Bakersfield. May operated a gas station near Taft. William Herbert May died on March 15, 1984, in the city where his life began.

Chapter 29
THE EARL OF OILDALE

Bakersfield, 1986

A standout pitcher for North High School, George Culver was scouted by a number of Major League teams. Despite a solid offer from the Philadelphia Phillies to sign after high school in 1961, Culver instead decided to pitch for Bakersfield College. He turned down an offer from the Phils, a $1,000 signing bonus and a $500 monthly salary to pitch for the Renegades, whose head baseball coach at the time was Gerry Collis, a man probably better known for his long tenure as head football coach at Bakersfield College. He took the offer to Collis, who at one time had played with the New York Yankees.

"He was the only one I knew who had played pro baseball," explained Culver. "He more or less recruited me. He said that if I would play for him for two years, I could get a better deal. I grew up without a father, and Gerry at Bakersfield College, along with Sam Barton at North High, were father figures to me and big influences, although I didn't think about such things at the time."

Collis was a rookie minor leaguer in 1952 with the Hutchinson (Kansas) Elks in the Western Association and with the Billings (Montana) Mustangs in the Pioneer League. Both were Class C entries affiliated with the Pittsburgh Pirates. He batted .261 in 57 games with Hutchinson and .323 in 21 games with Billings. He served a stint in the military and returned to pro baseball in 1956 as a New York Yankees farmhand with the Winston-Salem Twins in the Class B Carolina League. There, in 140 games, he batted 472 times with 119 hits for a .252 batting average, ending his two-year minor-league career.

Bakersfield College coach Gerry Collis (far right) was the presenter in 1968 when the Bakersfield Jockey Club named Culver Athlete of the Year. Bakersfield resident and National League umpire Bob Engel looks on. *Photograph courtesy George Culver.*

Culver had two years on the mound for the Renegades and wound up signing with the Yankees for $2,500 and a monthly salary equal to what the Phils had offered.

"More important," Culver pointed out, "was that I had the two years under Gerry and a chance to grow up a little bit. It turned out to be the best advice I ever received and the best decision I ever made."

"Gerry wouldn't let scouts talk to the players," Culver continued. "They had to go through him. All he told me was that teams were interested in me. Gerry was responsible for my reaching as far as I did in baseball. My definition of a good coach is one who continues to inspire excellence from his players long after his association with them has ended."

One might picture Culver as a schoolboy phenomenon with a blazing fastball, hurling aspirin tablets past batter after batter. But Culver, who has been described as having more moxie than talent, wasn't that kind of overpowering pitcher. "I used my intelligence," he said. "I never did throw very hard, but I got them out. I think the most strikeouts I had in a high school game was twelve. When I was thirteen or fourteen, I learned to throw a curve ball. That built up a lot of confidence, because at that age, you can strike out anyone with a curve. I tried to figure out a batter's weakness, throw strikes and throw strikes in the right spots."

Culver, who was born in Salinas and moved with his family to Delano at age two, later settled in Oildale and attended Standard School beginning in the eighth grade. He split his first minor-league season with teams in the Western Carolina and Florida State Leagues.

The Yankees, though, were unable to protect their young prospect from the newly initiated baseball draft system. The Cleveland Indians took the opening and landed Culver. "It was a break for me," he said. "The Yankees were loaded with talent. The Indians, because of how the draft worked, had to put me on their spring roster, and I was able to go to spring training with them."

It looked as if the door was now open to the Major Leagues, but Culver wasn't so sure. "I was kind of leery when I signed," he said. "I had no idea what I was getting into. I had been a success at whatever level I had played. Still, you have to prove yourself wherever you go. It was an opportunity. Cleveland had a poor team, and expansion had opened up more teams."

Shown here while with the Cincinnati Reds in 1968, the year he tossed a no-hitter, George Culver's heritage was later bared to a wide audience when Los Angeles Dodgers play-by-play man Vin Scully referred to him as the "Earl of Oildale." *Author's collection.*

Culver toiled in the minor leagues from 1964 to 1966, finally getting a promotion to the big time for a few games at the tail end of the 1966 campaign.

He had been a starting pitcher his entire career. That changed in 1967 when the Indians designated him for short reliever status. "I liked it, but I had no experience in that slot," he recalled. "It was my rookie year, and I went 7–3 with a few saves."

Cleveland traded Culver to Cincinnati in 1968 for outfielder Tommy Harper. Due to injuries on the Reds' pitching staff, Culver was pressed into the starting rotation. He responded in a big way by tossing a no-hitter against the Phillies. The Reds won the contest, 6–1, a more decisive score than Culver had been used to. "I pitched well for someone who ended with an 11–16 record," he said. "They [the Reds] scored a total of sixteen runs for me in my sixteen losses, and we had a good team—guys like Pete Rose, Vada Pinson, Tony Perez and Jim Maloney. I started, relieved and led the team in innings pitched."

In 1969, Culver continued in his dual role as starter and reliever when, midway through the season, he developed toxic hepatitis and had to sit out two months. "I don't know how I got it," he said. "I later found out it was a liver ailment."

It turned out to be the first of several physical problems.

After being traded again in 1970, this time to the St. Louis Cardinals for pitcher Ray Washburn, Culver won his first three decisions for the Cards while pitching with a bad elbow. He reported the injury, and an examination revealed he had bone chips in his pitching elbow.

"The chips were floating," said Culver. "The more I pitched, the worse it got. The Cardinals talked about an operation at the end of the year. Meanwhile, I didn't pitch much. Then I received a call from the Houston Astros telling me they had traded for me. I reported, and they asked me why I hadn't pitched much recently. I told them, and they became infuriated. I was damaged property. I pitched for them anyway and had an operation in the winter. I had two pretty good years with the Astros."

Two pretty good years? In 1972, his final year with Houston, Culver was one of the leading relievers in National League. "Houston used me as a middle and long man, probably the position I was best suited for. I was in the top ten in the league in just about all the important reliever categories."

A good year, huh? Fine, so how about a ticket to somewhere else? This time to the Los Angeles Dodgers. Culver, the "Pride of Oildale," packed up and moved again to join the Dodgers in 1973. "We were a real surprise," recalled Culver. "We got off to a great start. It was the first year the Dodgers had their infield of Steve Garvey, Davey Lopes, Ron Cey and Bill Russell. We had great chemistry on that team."

Culver stayed with the Dodgers until August, about the time the team began slipping in the standings. A Los Angeles newspaper columnist openly criticized the Dodgers for paving the way for Culver's departure.

Culver, apparently, was thought of as the catalyst who kept the Dodgers loose. "I did get a lot of publicity when the Dodgers let me go," he said. "The newspaper column was part of it, and I know for a fact that two players complained to manager Walter Alston about it."

Just how did Culver relate so well to the various personalities that made up the Dodgers?

"Well, we had just enough guys from Oklahoma—guys like Jim Brewer and Bill Russell—to let me be natural," he said. "I had a tape player, and on the bus and in the clubhouse, I'd put on Merle Haggard, Glen Campbell and Buck Owens—all country. As the season went on, even Alston liked it. The black guys enjoyed it, too. They gave up Motown for country. They'd sing right along. Team chemistry is a special thing."

While with the Dodgers, play-by-play man Vin Scully tagged Culver as the "Earl of Oildale."

Culver was picked up by the Phillies and assigned to the Toledo Mud Hens, a Triple A club.

"I hadn't worked out that much," he recalled. "Then my mother died. I wasn't in shape mentally or physically to play baseball."

He returned to the sport in 1975 to pitch in Japan. "I pitched one year for them," he said, "but not very well, and they didn't honor the second year of my contract. They still owe me $30,000. What can I do? Go over there and get involved in a lawsuit?"

Then, in 1976, Culver met Rosie, who was to become his third wife. Shortly after, he was named manager of the Bakersfield Outlaws, an independent entry in the Single A California League.

"Rosie is probably the only reason I'm still in baseball," Culver admitted. "She had a son, thirteen, and I got involved in working with him and other kids. They rekindled my fire. When you travel as much as I did and get traded a lot, you lose that competitive edge."

Culver, who has been a pitching coach for the Phillies the past five years, expects to be named the manager for the Phils' 1986 Double A team in Reading, Pennsylvania. "They're supposed to have one of their best crops of young players in years," Culver said, showing the enthusiasm of a Little League cleanup hitter.

In the meantime, Culver, a six-handicap golfer, is content to come to Bakersfield, visit with old friends and tee off on his favorite golf courses. From 1971 to 1981, he had his own local golf tournament. "I began going to Latin America for winter ball, and I wasn't able to put it [the golf tournament] on anymore," recalled Culver. "Something like that has to have continuity. The last few years, it became a fundraising tournament. We raised about $150,000 for worthwhile causes, and I'm proud of that."

Culver doesn't sound as if he plans on ever leaving Bakersfield on a permanent basis. "I've never found any place I'd rather be than here," he said. "I guess the most important reason is that I have so many friends here who are dear to me. And the fact I can play the Kern County golf courses for thirty-three dollars a month is a real steal."

Culver compiled a modest 48–49 career won-loss record while pitching all or parts of nine Major League seasons. The numbers, however, are of secondary importance to him. "I never felt I was destined to be a star," he said. "I had a dream, and I made the most of it. I've never fully appreciated it because it went by so fast. I had the thrill of pitching during an era when some of the greatest players of all time, at least twenty of them, either played with me or against me."

Afterword: Culver's longest baseball tenure was his eighteen years with the Philadelphia Phillies as a coach and manager at the AA and AAA levels. He now enjoys retirement with his wife, Rosie, and playing golf. He remains a popular figure in Bakersfield.

Chapter 30
THE INFAMOUS BAKERSFIELD OUTLAWS

Bakersfield, 1978

Question: What's the worst thing about managing a baseball team with
  pitchers who have a problem throwing strikes?
Answer: Going home late every night.

To the manager for the 1978 Bakersfield Outlaws, the team that could
not throw straight, the solution to the above question was a relatively
simple one. Though George Culver was thirty-four with a Major League
career now behind him, he still had his control.

With all the walks and wild pitches produced by his pitching corps, games
for the aptly named Outlaws lasted longer than normal.

Culver had a remedy for that. Whether winning or losing, he often took
over late mound chores with a main purpose in mind. "I pitched quite a bit,"
he said. "I wanted to get it over with and go home."

The Outlaws were a decent offensive team, with a team batting average of
.289, but fielding was also a problem. "That was another thing, we couldn't
field, either," said Culver. We did have some nice production from our local
players, most of whom were past their prime."

John Moncier, freshman baseball coach at South High, led the league
in losses. With a 4–16 pitching record, he still managed to have a modest
3.81 ERA. The Outlaws did not give him much run support, and sloppy
defensive play also contributed to several of those setbacks.

"Anything that was a negative statistic, we led the league in," Moncier
said. "George asked me to be his pitching coach, and I ended up pitching a

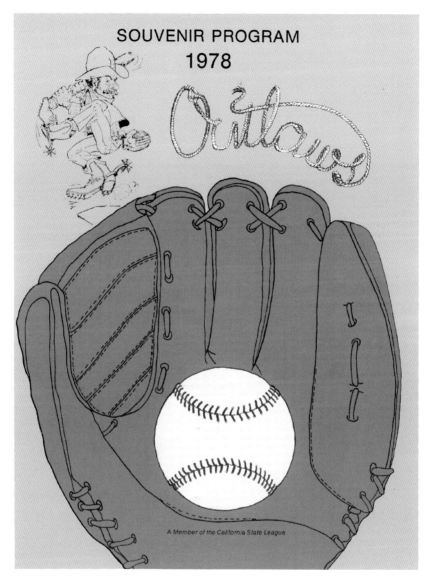

Manager Culver did his best in trying to tame the wildness exhibited by the pitching staff of the 1978 independent entry in the California League, the Bakersfield Outlaws. *Author's collection.*

bunch of innings. I had some pretty good years in the Twins organization until I tore an Achilles tendon. I had been out of baseball as a player for about five years. Three weeks into the season for the Outlaws, I think I was I was in the top three in the league in earned run average."

John Moncier, shown here as a minor-league pitching coach with the Philadelphia Phillies in 1984, had a league-worst 4–16 pitching record hurling for the 1978 Bakersfield Outlaws but still managed to maintain a rather respectable ERA. *Photograph courtesy John Moncier.*

Culver appointed Taft's Dan Beerbower as the infield coach. Beerbower was an all-star shortstop in the Florida State League and in the Cal League in 1973. He also pitched some in AA ball.

No starting pitcher had a winning record. The Outlaws finished last in the eight-team Cal League with a 48–92 ledger.

In spot duty, Culver sported a 2–0 won-loss record in twenty-three appearances. His ERA of 5.57 was below the team average of 6.20. He was, however, pelted for fifty-seven hits in forty-two innings. On the plus side, his strikeout to walk ratio of 38–16 and the fact he gave up only one home run are indicators of solid mound work. He did manage to uncork 6 wild pitches to contribute to a team total of 128.

Dan Walker served as general manager for team owner Rich Eglin. Some of the Outlaws, including catcher Ron Steele, played in the Kern County League for BC Chemicals, another business owned by Eglin. Steele made his pro baseball debut with the Outlaws. A West High graduate, he had played college ball at Fresno State.

The arrival of the independent Outlaws revived pro baseball careers for some regional players. Independent pro teams like to stock squads with as many locals as possible to cut down on costs, allowing locals to continue working their regular, non-baseball jobs.

Beerbower was originally drafted by the Baltimore Orioles in 1970 in the fourth round as an infielder right out of Kern County's Taft Union High School. In 1973, he became the property of the California Angels. He made it as high as AA ball with El Paso. The Angels gave him a brief shot as a pitcher with Quad Cities in 1976 before releasing him. Beerbower was one of the local bright spots for the inept Outlaws. He batted .469 (fifteen for thirty-two), played some at all four infield spots and was 3–3 on the mound through ninety-one innings.

Infielder Lance Garner came right off the Fresno State diamond. He attended North High and then played baseball at Bakersfield College, and during summers, he was a top player in the Kern County League. Others with area ties included infielder Leonard Morin (Highland High); first baseman Joe Dodder (Bakersfield Dodgers and Bakersfield resident); pitcher Gary Grunsky (Delano); outfielder Al Nichols (East Bakersfield High), formerly in the Reds organization; and Ron Valenti (baseball coach at Highland High).

The Chicago Cubs, San Diego Padres, Chicago White Sox and Seattle Mariners shipped players to fill the bulk of the team.

White Sox loanee Ronald Woods was the team's mound workhorse (189 innings), and at 13–13, he was the only hurler to post double-digit wins.

On loan from the San Diego Padres, Kevin Skahan came to the Outlaws from the Reno Silver Sox in early May with an 0–0 won-loss record and a 4.50 ERA. He made his first start on June 6 against the Salinas Angels. The six-foot-three, 195-pounder from Dodge City, Kansas, fired a two-hit shutout in the hot temperatures of a first-game doubleheader. "I want to get in the starting rotation and stay there,"

Skahan said. He had an earned run average of 3.00, fourth best in the league, last year at Walla Walla.

"He's valuable to us because he can throw strikes," said Culver, who did not have to emphasize the importance of that asset. The season total of 983 walks by Outlaws pitchers was 276 more free passes than the next highest team total.

Skahan married his college sweetheart, Janet, in March and lived in a camper on the parking lot of the ball field as a means to save money and help support his wife, who was still working on her college degree in Santa Barbara. He was one of the few Outlaws who were married.

A favorite ball shagger for the Outlaws was Sherman, Skahan's three-legged German shepherd.

Skahan finished the year 6–9 with a 5.80 ERA.

Three Chicago Cubs loanees posted good offensive numbers: Gene "Gary" Krug, first base (.318, 15 home runs, 103 RBIs); Jared Martin, outfield/first base (.325, 52 RBIs); Michael Thompson, infield (.313, 14 home runs, 80 RBIs). From the Chicago White Sox, there was infielder/outfielder Michael Johnson (.311, 12 home runs, 64 RBIs). Two other .300 hitters were unaffiliated: Nichols (.316, 7 home runs, 71 RBIs) and Terry Lee (.319, 13 home runs, 61 RBIs).

WHO IS RAY GAULT?

They raised their limbs like lifeless tools—
We were a ghastly crew.

A snippet of poetry from Samuel T. Coleridge's "Rime of the Ancient Mariner" could have served as the woeful words of Outlaws' helmsman Culver.

Robert Madden was 1–10 with an 8.90 ERA. A 1975 signee by the Chicago White Sox, Madden walked 143 batters in eighty-eight innings. He threw eleven wild pitches.

Ray Gault, at 2–10 with a 10.75 ERA, was worse. Gault was a walk machine, and he was wild to boot. He set a California League record on April 24, 1978, when he uncorked eight wild pitches in the second inning against Reno. He walked 156 batters in seventy-two innings, striking out 67. He threw thirty-three wild pitches.

Culver must have known he had a project when the hulking right-hander went 1–3 with a 13.91 ERA and walked forty-seven batters in just twenty-two innings the previous season with the Jersey City Indians in Double-A ball.

"Ray Gault had the strongest arm I've ever seen," said Moncier. "What really got me at the time was when he struck out thirteen batters against the Fresno Giants—and walked thirteen. Well, the next day he's playing burnout with an outfielder in front of the dugout."

Originally a Cardinals prospect, Gault's control problems were more mental than mechanical, Moncier suspects. "Part of his control problem was that he would be wound so tight when he pitched. You could hardly talk to him he would be so pumped."

The year's attendance for the Outlaws was 36,503, sixth best in the eight-team loop.

A highlight for the Outlaws had to be in regard to a game in Reno on August 25. In a twist to the normal script, the Outlaws defeated the Reno Silver Sox by a score of 30–14. In Outlaws-esque fashion, Reno's fielders committed nine errors, and their pitchers gave up fourteen walks.

Afterword: In a three-year minor-league career spanning 179 innings pitched, Florida native Gault walked 329 batters. His career ERA was 10.01. With a few more innings, Gault likely would have set all-time minor-league records for wildness. Even with a suspect résumé, Gault still had suitors. "After he left the Outlaws, I read where the Cubs signed him to a Triple-A contract," said Moncier. "When the guy with the Cubs was asked why they would sign someone to Triple-A who had problems in Single-A, he basically said if he can get the mental part down, he can pitch anywhere." Gault's stay with the Triple-A Wichita Aeros in 1979 under manager Jack Hiatt was brief and served as a finale to his pro career. Hiatt, incidentally, took his first breath in Bakersfield. In 1979, the final year of their two-year existence, manager Ron Mihal guided the Outlaws to a 63–77 season. The 1978 Outlaws enjoyed a reunion in Bakersfield on August 25, 2013. If their past serves as any kind of indicator, they had a wild time.

DALKOWSKI WOULD HAVE BEEN A GREAT OUTLAW

In all fairness to the Outlaws, pro independent baseball teams have problems affiliated teams do not. When players are performing badly at the minor-league level, suitable replacements for independent minor-league teams are hard to find, especially at the mid-season mark. Also, once a season has started and a team is playing poorly, those who could send players do not want to send prospects to a team of "losers." In 1978, the Outlaws were one of just three minor-league teams in the nation operating without a working commitment with a Major League franchise.

As wild a pitcher as the fastballing Gault was, a former Cal Leaguer with Bakersfield ties threw even harder and with less command of his pitches. In the late 1950s and early '60s, Steve Dalkowski launched a baseball at speeds upward of 120 miles per hour—so goes the legend. The bespectacled left-hander had not only the stories told about his legendary speed but also the strikeouts to prove it. In 1960 with Stockton, he set a California League record with 262 strikeouts in 170 innings, walking an equal 262 batters in the process.

The character "Nuke" LaLoosh in the 1988 film *Bull Durham* was modeled after Dalkowski by screenwriter and director Ron Shelton. "LaLoosh" could just as well have been "LaLush" due to his notorious abuse of alcohol. Dalkowski's pro baseball career ended in 1966. Somewhere in that immediate time frame, he married a Bakersfield schoolteacher. The marriage did not last long.

Dalkowski lived in cheap hotels and frequented the bars and liquor stores in East Bakersfield along Baker and Sumner Streets. He was arrested many times for bar fights. Various individuals looked after his welfare the best they could; one was Larry Press, sports editor at the daily *Californian* newspaper. In the early 1980s, Dalkowski was residing at the Hotel Bakersfield, an old hostelry situated in a tenderloin region on East Nineteenth Street. Across from the elderly hotel sat The Mint tavern, and just down the street was Roy Lewis's Cigar and Liquor Store. For a number of years during early crop season, Press would post an alert in his sports column about the availability of Steve Dalkowski, a man down on his luck and seeking a job as a field hand.

OUTLAWS CAUSE PRO WOMEN'S SOFTBALL TEAM TO CANCEL SEASON

To further add to its notoriety, the mere existence of the team delivered a knockout punch to the Bakersfield Aggies, a Women's Professional Softball Association team.

The Aggies had played an inaugural season at Sam Lynn Ball Park in 1977, but with the arrival of the Outlaws in 1978, they would have been forced to play home games in the afternoon. They opted to drop out of the WPSA for the 1978 season and reenter in 1979. They dropped out never to play again.

The Aggies' only season was the second year for the league. When the Phoenix/Arizona Bird dissolved, Bakersfield was awarded the franchise and team players. The Aggies added some local talent, including Carrie Fimbres and Linda Belcher. The star of the league was pitcher Joan Joyce of the Connecticut Falcons.

Billy Carter headlined a kickoff dinner at the Rio Bravo Tennis Ranch in May 1977 to introduce the Aggies to the press. A cowboy hat sitting atop a softball was the team logo.

Chapter 31

HAIL, HAIL, THE GREAT JOHNNY CALLISON

Bakersfield, 1986

John Wesley Callison moved with his family to Bakersfield in 1944. He became an all-around star athlete at East Bakersfield High, especially in baseball, which led to his signing with the Chicago White Sox in 1957. With his combination of speed and power, he drew early comparisons to Mickey Mantle.

The Pale Hose assigned the eighteen-year-old with the smooth swing to his hometown Bakersfield Bears of the Class C California League.

Callison signed for a $7,000 bonus, and some reports say he received an additional $3,000 under the table. At the time, his family lived on Jeffrey Street in a small 1940s house in the northeast region of the city. His father, Virgil, worked as a laborer, and his mother, Wilda, was a maid at General Hospital. In addition to the White Sox, Callison played ten years with the Philadelphia Phillies and finished his career with short stopovers with the Chicago Cubs and New York Yankees. Hitters ran the bases with caution due to Callison's cannon-like throwing arm.

The Hollywood-handsome Callison totaled sixteen years in the big leagues, hitting .264 with 226 home runs and 2,934 total bases over the course of his career.

An All-Star in 1962, 1964 and 1965, he won the All-Star Game MVP honor in 1964. He hit over twenty-five home runs three times and over thirty home runs twice. Twice he scored one hundred runs, and twice he drove in one hundred runs. In 1966, he led the league in doubles, and in 1962 and 1965, he led the league in triples. In 1964, Callison was runner-up to Ken Boyer of the St. Louis Cardinals for the annual league MVP award.

A super right fielder with all the tools, Johnny Callison is considered by a majority to be the best baseball player Bakersfield has ever produced. *Author's collection.*

Callison was one of the best right fielders of his time. Each year from 1962 to 1965, Callison led the league in outfield assists, and in 1963, 1964 and 1968, he led the league in fielding percentage at right field. Callison ranks seventy-ninth all-time in outfield assists and twenty-ninth all-time in fielding percentage in right field.

Not quite a Hall of Fame player during his career, he was arguably the best baseball player to ever come out of Bakersfield.

Born in Qualls, Oklahoma, in 1939, Callison married his high school sweetheart, Dianne Moore. They had three daughters: Lori, Cindi and Sherri. Both of his parents, Virgil and Wilda, passed away in Bakersfield, Wilda in 1972 and Virgil in 1977.

Afterword: A regular at Phillies fantasy camps in Florida after his retirement, Callison died from cancer and heart-related problems on October 12, 2006, at age sixty-seven. He had lived in the same house in Glenside, Pennsylvania, for forty-five years.

ART WILLIAMS: "THE JACKIE ROBINSON OF UMPIRES"

Two National League umpires resided in Bakersfield: Art Williams and Bob Engel.

As a right-handed pitcher in 1953, Williams was the first black player in the Detroit Tigers organization. He received a $100 bonus for signing and was assigned to the Tigers' Class A farm team in his hometown of Bakersfield.

Williams progressed quite favorably on the mound until an arm injury curtailed his career in 1957. He later reflected on how some bad advice from a Tigers boss led to overuse of his arm and how the overall experience left him feeling bitter about the game.

Taking a job with the Bakersfield Sanitation Department, he soon advanced to supervisor. He was there for twelve years while he and his wife, Shirley, raised five children. One of those kids, Art Williams Jr., started playing Little League ball, and Williams volunteered as an umpire. In no time at all, he moved up to high school and college umpiring, developing much respect in Kern County for his abilities. He was inspired to take up umpiring after watching veteran arbiter Tudy McDaniel make the calls on the many dusty diamonds in Kern County.

With the encouragement of Major League Baseball, which was seeking to add a black umpire to its fold, Williams spent six weeks at an umpire school in Florida. Bob Engel, a National League umpire who lived in Bakersfield, had recommended the school to Williams. The only other black umpire—the first and only one—was Emmett Ashford of the American League. Ashford was set to retire soon.

On September 18, 1972, after three years in the minors, Williams became the first black umpire in the National League. Over a six-year career, he umpired 806 MLB games, including the 1975 National League Championship Series.

Williams was scrutinized harshly in a unique and controversial book about umpires by author Lee Gutkind, who in 1974 traveled with the umpiring crew of Doug Harvey (crew chief), Nick Colosi, Harry Wendelstedt and Williams. The book was titled *The Best Seat in Baseball, but You Have to Stand: The Game as Umpires See It.*

Williams was fired in 1977 for what the league office said was "incompetence after many warnings." Despite more than a dozen white umpires backing him in a petition, the termination held up. Baseball had struck a sour note with him once more.

While working as a Bakersfield city bus driver, Williams passed away at age forty-four in 1979 from complications due to a brain seizure. At one time, there was a movement to name a street after him in Bakersfield, where he grew up after being born in Arkansas. The semipro Kern County League was renamed the Art Williams League in his honor. Considering that he was the first black umpire in the National League and the first black player for the Detroit Tigers, you could say he was a "double Jackie Robinson."

One of Art's sons, Brian Keith Williams, was a South High product drafted by the Dodgers in 1981. Brian was in the minors for six seasons (1981–86) and had a career

Art Williams broke the MLB color barrier when he became the National League's first black umpire in 1972. *Bob Elias Sports Hall of Fame.*

batting average of .301. He hit .340 in 1985 for the Bakersfield Dodgers in 471 at-bats. Amazingly, with his talent, he never went higher than Single-A.

VETERAN UMPIRE BOB ENGEL IN UNFORTUNATE, BIZARRE EPISODE

Bob Engel was a common voice on Bakersfield radio after he announced his retirement from umpiring in July 1990. He had previously been charged with and sentenced in Bakersfield Municipal Court for stealing more than four thousand baseball cards from a Target store in Bakersfield. He was placed on three years' probation by the court and ordered to perform forty hours of community service and seek counseling. Through his attorney, Engel pleaded no contest to the charges.

Engel umpired in the National League from 1965 to 1990. He worked four Major League Baseball All-Star Games and the 1972, 1979 and 1985 World Series. In all, Engel umpired 3,630 MLB contests.

In an interview with a *Sports Illustrated* writer in 1987, Engel said he wanted to become an umpire when he was a schoolboy in Bakersfield and took a job as a bellboy. Engel said he noticed how the umpires who stayed at the hotel got all the pretty girls and had a ton of fun.

Chapter 32
GREG ARTZ: DRAG-BOAT RACER ON A MISSION

Taft, 1978

Drag-boat racing is America's fastest-growing and most exciting sport. So says Greg Artz, intent on enduring the dangerous physical risks and the financial premiums involved on his way to a personal high-water mark as a top nitro fueler.

The nitro class is the fastest among exotic fuelers, but presently, Artz is seeking financial assistance to back standard quarter-mile sprints in his eighteen-foot, blown-alcohol hydroplane, in which he competes in the second-fastest hydro class.

At $1 per gallon, fifty gallons of methanol fuel will last Artz for "two or three races." When he moves up to the nitro class, nitromethane will cost him $10 a gallon, or $500 for a fifty-gallon drum, from which the contents will be consumed in two contests.

Artz explains that unlike gasoline, methanol, a pure chemical, has no hydrocarbons and that no detonation is experienced, amounting to a tremendous thrust and an unmatched thrill for the driver.

"A hydro will leave harder, but a nitro comes on hard at top end. It almost stops your heart," said Artz, a husky six-footer with two years of racing experience. "It's a real rush for the first seven seconds. After that, it starts costing you hundreds of dollars."

A hydro-class sponsor would need to put up about $15,000 a year to keep Artz pushing at his maximum. To run nitro, the dollars increase to the $50,000 to $60,000 neighborhood.

Drag-boat racer Greg Artz shoots the water at nearly 170 miles per hour in his Nighthawk hydroplane. *Photograph courtesy Greg Artz.*

"The sponsor, ideally, should be someone who is free and who likes the excitement—and there's nothing more exciting than boat racing," said Artz. "You're not sitting in a hot grandstand or steaming over hot asphalt as a spectator, either. You've got shade trees, grass and lots of pretty girls in bikinis to keep you company. I need sponsors—and not just for me, because I'm going to put every cent into it no matter what. But with a little backing, I can go harder. I want to do it to be a part of something."

Artz recently placed third at Lake Ming in a sanctioned drag event that paid $2,500 to the top finisher. He is firmly dedicated to his cause and does not think he would buckle under the pressure of those drivers with more money at their disposal. "I'm competing against guys who spend $50,000 a year, and I've squeezed them a few times. They sure don't like it since I'm a nobody."

He spent $12,000 last year on engine maintenance, which included major block work. A bare block alone costs $3,000. Five quarter-mile runs, or one day at the races, is the limit before the engine needs to be "gone through," costing $100 to $300. Artz's income comes from running his dad's liquor store.

At G-force speeds, Artz's speedboat can leave "rooster tails" three hundred feet long and waves twenty-five to thirty-five feet high. *Photograph courtesy Greg Artz.*

The 1,600-horsepower engine powering Artz's Nighthawk is "Chevy designed" and has an $11,000 price tag. The entire rig would cost $20,000 to replace. "I can't figure out why they say 'Chevy designed' when the only things Chevrolet are the heads, valves and crankshaft," said Artz, who built and sold over a dozen pleasure boats before entering racing. "The engine is really quite detailed. It alone would involve a great deal of discussion."

His Nighthawk has a $1,400 pearlescent paint job and "what looks like a bird from Aztec Airlines" running down its sides. The name Nighthawk does not appear on the boat, and there's a reason for that. "You put a name on your boat, and everybody becomes familiar with seeing that name. When you get a sponsor, they want their own name on it," said Artz, who wishes he had such problems.

The race boat does have "Special thanks to Tom Henderson, Everett Binkley and Gerald Hudson" painted on the aft side, the names stacked vertically. A mobile (at times, very mobile) advertisement streams horizontally across the back: "Bill Brasher and Son Trucking."

"Henderson and Binkley let me use the machine shop at CCI Sales and Service, Hudson helps me order special parts from Tasco and Brasher pays

$100 a month for his advertisement," said Artz. "I'd never make it without these guys, but I need some big sponsors because the sport is breaking me to the point of no return. It's not a toy I'm playing with. This is the most dangerous sport there is, and I put my life on the line every time I get into this thing."

David White, the only other professional drag-boat racer in Taft, is Artz's "motor man," and Bill Standridge of Standridge-Ward in Bakersfield takes care of the tune-ups.

"David helps me wrench my boat, and I wrench his," said Artz. "Standridge hasn't burned a piston for me yet, which is easy to do with these engines." The majority of the mechanic work Artz handles alone. "I've stayed up all night working on the engine for just two weekend runs," he said. "I do it on a natural high. I don't believe in dope. I'll drink a beer, but you can't afford to be fuzzyheaded out there. I'm running 166 miles per hour, and I hope to get in the 170s with my new blower."

At those speeds, it is not unusual for the Nighthawk to leave rooster tails three hundred feet long and waves twenty-five to thirty-five feet high. Waves and ripples are part of the dangers for the racers, along with any debris that may be in the waters.

"At Phoenix, they're going to start running at night," said Artz. "They'll have lights underwater so that spectators can see the wave silhouettes. It's the first time ever for such a thing. An Indian chief bought the place and came up with the idea. It's south of Phoenix near the Gila River Indian Reservation."

Artz explained that the underwater lights will silhouette the waves and thus present a dramatic and spectacular picture for those on dockside.

Around 240 boats, about 40 from the eastern United States, are expected to compete at Lake Ming in Bakersfield on May 20 when Artz next picks up the challenge. Sanctioned boat drags are held all over California, and in addition to the ready cash prizes, money is also split at the end of the year based on points totals. After Lake Ming, Artz may miss some sleep getting ready for the following weekend in Phoenix. Local races cost Artz $300 per year, including entry fees. Going on the road increases expenses. "I'm going all over this year," he said. "Back east, this sport is going over big. My plan hasn't changed. I plan to keep on squeezing the big guys and to come up with a sponsor. You'd have to say it is part ego, but the sport is in my blood."

Afterword: In case of a spill in his speedboat, Artz, a champion swimmer at Bakersfield College, was well prepared. He also raced dragsters on the asphalt and with great results. Today, he owns and operates various businesses in Taft.

THE NEED FOR SPEED

Another Taftian showed a high degree of interest in street machines and super speeds of the salt flats. Lee Kelley graduated from Taft High in 1960. In 1968, Kelley set a C-Class land-speed record at Bonneville in *Hot Rod* magazine's special Oldsmobile. He also drove modified production machines in drag races and was an avid off-road enthusiast. Kelley joined Peterson Publishing Company in Los Angeles in 1968 as a technical feature writer for *Hot Rod*. He became editor of the publication in the late 1970s.

ABOUT THE AUTHOR

As a high school athlete in Kansas, Bryce Martin lettered in four sports: baseball, football, track and basketball. He was an All-Southeast Kansas centerfielder in American Legion baseball. He served in the U.S. Marine Corps as a platoon guide during the Vietnam era. He graduated from Cal State Bakersfield University with a BA degree in English. Martin is likely the only journalist to have worked for all three Kern County daily newspapers: the *Taft Daily Midway Driller* (now the *Midway Driller*), the *Bakersfield Californian* and the *Ridgecrest Daily Independent*. In addition, he contributed sports features to many Kern County magazines and periodicals, including *Kern Tab*, *CB Trader*, *Spotlight Bakersfield* and others. His sports articles found print in *Kansas City Magazine*, *Business Nashville Magazine* and *Maury County Archives*

Courtesy of Ridgecrest Daily Independent.

(Tennessee). In the early 2000s, he contributed regular feature articles to Jim Rome's website (Cyber Fishwrap). He played baseball for Taft in the Kern County League and fast-pitch softball for the Dunker Ducks in the Kern County Recreation League and served as a high school baseball umpire in Bakersfield. In early editions of *The Sports Collector's Bible*, Martin gained recognition as a trading card and memorabilia collector. His biggest thrill in sports was meeting his hero, Mickey Mantle, as a boy at the slugger's home in Commerce, Oklahoma. He still has the baseball Mantle signed in 1955. Divorced, he has a daughter, Marcy Ann, who lives in San Diego.